W9-AFX-111

ADVANCE PRAISE FOR
CAPITALIZE ON YOUR SUCCESS

"Capitalize on Your Success provides an excellent primer for any aspiring entrepreneur seeking funding to create a high potential start-up. Julie Garella, who has been there and done that in the world of venture finance shares the reality of what it takes to get deals done on the road of value creation."

—Nan Langowitz, D.B.A.
Director, The Center for Women's Leadership at Babson College

"Julie Garella takes a complex topic and boils it down to pragmatic and insightful advice that goes beyond the commentary of a traditional how-to book. This is a great book that will speak to entrepreneurs everywhere."

—Jacqueline D. Reses
Partner, Apax Partners

"I have seen Julie Garella in action. She takes her wealth of experience and provides a step-by-step guide to the process of increasing business valuation and raising capital. Nothing is sacrosanct as Julie walks us through the art as well as the science of a deal—the pitfalls, the tactics, and the hidden rules to success. She is a master at laying the groundwork so that we can reach our business goals."

—June Rokoff
Cofounder The Commonwealth Institute, former senior vice president, Lotus Development Corporation

"Are you a lifestyle maker or empire builder? Garella shares her extensive experience and wisdom on this and vividly illuminates critical concepts every growth-oriented entrepreneur needs to know—valuation, capital strategies, and the anatomy of a deal. I read it in one sitting!"

—Tamara Monosoff, Ed.D.
Founder & CEO, Mom Inventors, Inc., Author of The Mom Inventors Handbook: How To Turn Your Great Idea into the Next Big Thing

"Capitalize on Your Success is a great guide to just that—in ways that affect you personally, professionally, and financially. Julie Garella has been a superb model for this formula for success, having done that at every juncture of her career and life."

—Mylle Mangum
Chairman and CEO, IBT Enterprises, LLC

"Julie Garella is a valuable asset to America's economy. She has long pioneered entrepreneurship in the United States and has been a courageous endorser and promoter of the untapped resources of American women. This book will be an even more important step in helping all business owners reach their full potential in today's business world."

—Barbara J. Friedman
President of Licensing, Liz Claiborne, Inc.

CAPITALIZE
ON YOUR
SUCCESS

The Ultimate Guide to
GETTING THE MONEY,
GROWING THE BUSINESS,
and
DOING THE DEAL

JULIE GARELLA

KAPLAN PUBLISHING

Editorial Director: Jennifer Farthing
Acquisitions Editor: Karen Murphy
Production Editor: Karen Goodfriend
Typesetter: Janet Schroeder
Cover Designer: Design Solutions

© 2007 by Julie Garella

Published by Kaplan Publishing,
a division of Kaplan, Inc.

Printed in the United States of America

07 08 09   10 9 8 7 6 5 4 3 2 1

Library of Congress Cataloging-in-Publication Data

Garella, Julie.
    Capitalize on your success : the ultimate guide to getting the money, growing the business, and doing the deal / Julie Garella.
      p. cm.
      ISBN-13: 978-1-4195-8330-8
      ISBN-10: 1-4195-8330-1
1. Women-owned business enterprises. 2. New business enterprises–
Management. I. Title.
  HD2341.G27 2006
  658.15'224–dc22
  2006027369

Kaplan Publishing books are available at special quantity discounts to use for sales promotions, employee premiums, or educational purposes. Please call our Special Sales Department to order or for more information at 800-621-9621, ext. 4444, e-mail kaplanpubsales@kaplan.com, or write to Kaplan Publishing, 30 South Wacker Drive, Suite 2500, Chicago, IL 60606-7481.

To the entrepreneurial spirit in all of us

CONTENTS

FOREWORD

by **GAIL EVANS**,
author of *Play Like a Man, Win Like a Woman*

I met Julie Garella when I served on the advisory board of her banking firm, McColl Garella, and observed how knowledgeable and articulate she was. What especially impressed me about Julie was how important she thought it was that owners of closely held businesses understand how to value their companies, where to go for growth capital, why it was necessary to work their business plans—including their exit strategies—every day, and generally play the game the way the Fortune 500 companies do. There's no mystery to doing these deals, Julie would constantly remind everyone, there was simply a lack of information.

It was fascinating to see how the people I referred to her always came back with a similar comment. Whether it was an assignment she could bring to fruition or not, they were pleased with the way she could get them comfortable with the process, the language, and the entire experience of raising capital and doing a deal, because they always exclaimed how they never knew it worked that way!

So it follows that Julie would want to share what she knows with a larger audience. Now a senior vice president and director of business development with Citigroup's Capital Strategies Group, she encounters owners of closely held business every day and hears the same problems that she addresses in this book. In *Capitalize On Your Success* Julie has taken the rules of finance and deal making for growing your business and boiled it down so that you will understand what really goes on in the minds of the empire builder, lender, investor, and buyer and how you should be thinking about your business plan every day.

When Julie told me she wanted to write a book based on her experiences and the many requests she gets after her speeches and public presentations to make her information more widely available, I thought, terrific! because those of you who know me know that my philosophy is to share the knowledge so others don't have to shoulder the same struggles.

In the pages that follow you will learn the language and the process, and a bit about what to expect when you venture in the world of corporate finance and M&A. It's a fact that anyone who has successfully started, grown, and sold a business will tell you: There is a set of rules and special language that applies.

Consider this book your guide to that process and rejoice in the fact that you've found a mentor who can demystify a very demanding but ultimately very rewarding process.

Gail Evans

Author of *Play Like a Man, Win Like a Woman*

August 2006

ACKNOWLEDGMENTS

So many people have helped me throughout my career and provided inspiration as I wrote this book that it's hard to know where to begin, but it all started with Arthur Monroe. While trying to recruit me to join his firm, Robinson Humphrey, he helped me overcome my fear of math by showing me how the discipline is just puzzles with numbers, and he convinced me to try my hand in the financial services arena. I'm also grateful to Walter Jameson, who taught me how to market smart and think like one of the boys.

I also want to acknowledge Hugh McColl, who put me on the map; Mylle Mangum, who always seems to check in at the right times, and is living proof you can be a big deal in business and a kind person too; Gail Evans, whose unique perspective keeps me on track—always; Caroline Gundeck, who gave me the opportunity to share my thoughts and voice with hundreds of business owners around the country; and my editorial consultant, Susan A. Schwartz, who nimbly worked my words and kept my voice. Thanks also to my Kaplan editor, Karen Murphy, for her enthusiastic comments about early drafts of the chapters that confirmed I was on the right track.

Kaplan's agreement to publish this book came during an especially challenging time in my personal life. I was winding up McColl Garella, wrapping up my life in Charlotte, North Carolina, and beginning a new life in New York City. I would not have been able to do it all, plus write this book, if it were not for the support and encouragement from my friends, Elyn Dortch and Megan Lambert. I owe both of them many thanks for believing in me, and cheering me on to the end.

INTRODUCTION

The idea for writing this book came one day when I was giving an interview to *Fortune Magazine*. We were talking about what is I *really* do. The writer wasn't asking me tactically what I did in terms of deal doing, but practically: How I mesh what I know about Mergers and Acquisitions and the Capital Markets to bring them to light for business owners. I answered the question by saying that on my next business card I was going to change my title from Managing Director to Translator because what I really did, every day, all day long was translate: What did the private equity firm really say when they delivered their term sheet? Why didn't the bank think they could make the type of loan the client was asking for? How was a company likely to be valued?

Until recently, I owned my own investment banking boutique together with Hugh McColl, the former chairman of Bank of America. We had a niche focus on women-owned and run companies. The genesis of the firm came from traveling the country talking to business owners about how they started their companies, what they did to grow the business, and what their exit strategies were. When we asked how they started their company we never heard that they acquired an ongoing concern or spun a division from a corporation or, for that matter, that they wrote a full-blown business plan and developed a financial mode—it was always that they bootstrapped: mortgaged the house, maxed out the credit cards, cashed in the retirement plan, and started from scratch. On the growth front, universally the business owners told us that they were growing organically, weren't using outside capital or looking for acquisition targets, and as for an exit strategy there wasn't one—several women even said that their exit was to die at their desks!

What I came to realize was that there was a knowing-versus-doing gap between the business owners, the capital markets, and the deal doers. And there wasn't really a place a business owner could turn to that explained in plain English the way things worked in deal land.

Over the years I have had the opportunity to speak to groups of business owners all over the country. Many times these were situations in which I'd be able to sit and listen to the issues that these businesses, their owners, and management were struggling with. Oftentimes they were emotional, with the business owner questioning what it was they really wanted from their business—it was those conversations that sparked Chapter 1.

Many times I'd be listening to a business owner, desperate for growth capital, who was spending their most precious resource—time—running around talking to investors and coming back empty-handed. Why? Pride of ownership. Not understanding how valuation works was getting in their way, so I've tackled that in Chapter 2.

I've often been accused of being a shark. Not because I'm prowling the waters but because I'm the type of person that has to keep swimming forward to feel alive. Growing a business requires constant movement too, but lots of activity in the wrong direction and without the right results makes no sense. Chapter 3 addresses the choices you'll have to make along the way to ensure a solid foundation and position yourself for future growth and expansion. I also share a useful exercise called a SWOT analysis to help you navigate crossroads as you come to them.

Money was another theme that came up over and over again. Mostly I found that entrepreneurs, especially those who had risked it all to get the business up and running, were not comfortable using other people's money, be it debt or equity. They were so used to sweating it out that it became their comfort zone. Chapters 4 and 5 were developed to open your eyes to the vast financial resources available and to provide some clues as to how investors and lenders think so you're not opening yourself up to unnecessary rejection if you decide to move down the path of raining outside capital.

If there was one story that repeated itself over and over, it was about the deal that got away. What I love about working with entrepreneurs is that they are true optimists. That glass is *always* at least half full! I think that is why so many people have such a hard time deciding when to pass the torch: You've birthed the business and built it and of course you can keep doing this forever. Unfortunately, after they let the opportunity go is when most business owners wish they knew more about timing, evaluating an offer, and how to know if they were getting a good deal. Chapters 6, 7, and 8 are all about understanding when the time is right to let go, or at least take some chips off the table, how the deal process works, and who to turn to for help. And since in business as in life it's all about communication I've included a glossary of terms to help you learn the language.

I currently work for Citigroup Capital Strategies, a division of Citigroup Global Markets Inc., and travel the country meeting with Smith Barney financial advisors and their clients. It's an interesting time for business owners. Private equity funds have raised an unprecedented amount of capital and I'll go so far as to say there's probably more capital available to fund growth or buy closely held businesses than there are good businesses available for sale or investment. Interest rates continue to remain at historic lows, allowing attractive leverage that gets deals done, and capital gains tax rates favor business owners who want to sell or take chips off the table.

All in all we have a perfect storm for you the business owner to *Capitalize On Your Success*.

Julie Garella
August 2006

CHAPTER ONE

Lifestyle Maker or Empire Builder?

I chose to start the book off with this subject because frankly, if you read it and decide you are a lifestyle maker, you need not read on. Lifestyle makers simply will not be able to execute the strategies described in the following chapters because they are in business for a separate set of reasons. This is not a commentary on which is better; it is simply a reality check. The reason the "big boys" do the deal is because they think like an empire builder. To see which one you are, read on.

Whether you are a lifestyle maker or an empire builder, chances are you started out like all successful entrepreneurs—with a good idea and lots of energy. As your company has grown and matured, you have found yourself at certain forks in the road. The personal and emotional factors that go into making the decisions at these moments are what determine into which category you fall.

FACTOR NUMBER ONE: YOUR PLAN

When I travel around the country and speak with owners of closely held businesses, I always ask the same set of questions:

- How did you start your business?
- How are you growing your business?
- What is your exit strategy?

What is stunning to me is that no matter which city I'm in—Boston, Dallas, New York, Hartford, or Raleigh—I always hear the same answers. When asked how they came to be business owners, the universal answer is *by accident.* Almost always, businesses are started due to a change in the owner's personal life, such as job loss, parenthood, divorce, or the illness or death of a parent or spouse.

In answering the second question—How are you growing your business?—I never hear that these entrepreneurs are growing through acquisition or using outside capital for expansion. In fact, many of them have no plan whatsoever for growth. Instead, I'd hear that their companies are bootstrapped. The growth is happening but not because there is a strategy; that is just the way it is going.

As for using outside capital, that was unheard of. In fact, I heard just the opposite. Most owners had not thought about it, and wouldn't know how to get it or what to do with it. These business owners were proud that they were debt free, even if that kept their businesses from reaching the next level of maturity. I often hear that it is difficult to obtain a line of credit from the bank, so they just don't bother to try. Almost universally, these entrepreneurs report that they liked owning 100 percent of their companies. The concept of owning a smaller slice of something really large wasn't an idea with which they were particularly comfortable.

Their answers to my final question about exit strategy were often the most revealing of a true disconnect between reality and what they want in terms of controlling their financial future. These business owners have no exit or succession strategy—I guess they are planning to die on the job! It would seem to me that if you were interested in being in control of your future, particularly from a financial standpoint, there would be a plan—a strategy—and you would work toward the end game each and every day. That is what empire builders do.

If you are reading along, nodding, and thinking, "That sounds just like me," then you might have fallen into the lifestyle maker trap.

Empire builders think big and purposefully. Many may have started their companies out of circumstance, much like a lifestyle maker, but they have a strategy and a plan that they work toward every single day. They understand how to create wealth for themselves, though this is most often a by-product of success rather than the purpose of the business. Empire builders understand the resources available to them—other people's money (OPM), human capital, professional relationships—and they know how to use them to advance their business plan.

Empire builders understand that it is actually *less* risky to use outside capital in order to grow a business, because it means that their own capital is not 100 percent committed, and therefore at risk. The whole concept of using and obtaining outside capital will be discussed at length in Chapter 5, but it is worth discussing here the psychological aspects that pertain to the two different types of business owners.

One of the observations that interests me is the way business owners make decisions when it is their money at risk versus someone else's money. Like anyone who is strapped for cash, the undercapitalized business owner tends to think small and conservatively, doing only what is absolutely necessary at that moment to get by. Now I am not advocating reckless spending, but I do believe that proper capitalization is the key to strong execution of a business model. When the money being spent to execute a strategy is not all yours, it forces you to build a business case for each decision in order to be accountable. This method works well if you have mentally separated your personal identity from the business objectives. However, if you are making decisions based on emotional attachments, lifestyle issues, or constraints, and not on sound business practices, you will find yourself tormented by the first tough decision you are forced to make to achieve your business objective.

The other issue surrounding the development of a plan and capitalizing yourself properly is that you run far less risk of personal peril. You will notice that people who are financially secure run their companies in a totally different way than those whose number one concern is making payroll. I am a big advocate of business owners taking some cash off the table as soon as they can to secure a nest egg. Similarly, if you are involved with a bank, you need to make sure you are working toward removing those personal guarantees as quickly as possible. Better yet, try not to have them in the first place (more on this in Chapter 4).

Empire builders understand that it is easier to run an empire than a village. An empire has a leadership structure, resources, and teams in place that can continue to execute the business plan through times of change. If you don't believe me, ask anyone who has grown a business to a meaningful size whether it was easier to manage at $200 million or $2 million in revenue. My guess is they will tell you that the larger company is much easier and ultimately less stressful, because with the larger company, they have resources that include other people to do the things they don't want to do!

FACTOR NUMBER TWO: EMOTIONS

How do you view your employees? Are they family, friends, business associates, or equity partners? Can you separate the personal relationship from the business relationship? This emotional component is not be confused with developing a culture. Many companies have strong employee loyalty and close-knit cultures at the same time. Their owners have been able mentally to separate their personal relationships from what is necessary to execute their business plan. If you see your employees as friends and family, you may fall victim to unnecessary guilt and emotional risk when it comes time to make a decision that may cause them to lose their jobs, such as acquiring another firm.

Consider the following situation. You have owned your company for several years and are ready to expand. After thoughtful analysis, you determine that growth through acquisition is going to be the easiest way to achieve your goal. Luckily for you, one of your prime competitors in a neighboring marketplace has just put itself on the block, and after proper due diligence, you determine that the acquisition makes sense. Your CFO points out that while there is very little customer overlap, there is a good bit of personnel overlap, but you should be able to generate even greater financial synergies by eliminating the duplication. As you move through the process, you determine that the sales manager of the company you are acquiring has a much stronger track record and more experience than your sales manger. Clearly, you don't need two sales managers. However, you just came back from a weeklong vacation with your sales manager and her family. She's been with you from the start, and even though you know you'd be better off with the guy from the other company, you just don't have the guts, energy, heart, stomach, or whatever it takes to either demote her or, even worse, let her go.

Over the coming weeks, your conscience weighs so heavily on you that you decide to discuss the situation internally. Seeking a consensus before you make a move seems like the right way to go. So, what happens? First, all of the employees you discuss the situation with immediately panic as they think, "What about me? Is my job secure?" Second, they begin to advise you based not on your business plan but what's in it for them. Finally, after much deliberation, you determine that the stress just isn't worth it: you were pretty happy and making good money before, so you let the opportunity pass you by.

Decisions from the Other Side of the Desk

Emotions don't only play into less-than-savvy decision making at the point of acquisition or potential sale of the company. Being too attached to your business can affect how you grow your company and whether that company will be investment-worthy or salable down the road. Making decisions from a place of relative detachment isn't being cold or unfeeling. After all, you do it all the time with your personal portfolio and never miss a night's sleep. If investments aren't growing, you divest. If those in charge of your investments are not successful in making them grow, you look for someone who will. And, if a new opportunity comes along that you believe will fuel wealth accumulation, you seize it. The same rules apply to your business—without guilt, anxiety, or compromise.

As hard as it is sometimes, you need to sit on the other side of the desk and regain your perspective. Recognize that the company you built is the most lasting—and potentially most lucrative—investment you own.

Quick Quiz: Are You Making Emotion-Based Business Decisions?

- Have you ever resisted firing a difficult or unproductive employee because he or she was your friend or because of the employee's personal circumstances?
- Would you be willing to let go of your entire management team if it meant increasing the salability of your enterprise?

- Are raises and bonuses commensurate with the company's success in any given year?
- Have you ever passed up a business opportunity because of how it would affect your employees (i.e., relocating offices farther from their homes)?

If you run your business like a family or a club, you could be a lifestyle maker.

FACTOR NUMBER THREE: IDENTITY

Who are you? I often tell people to think of an egg carton. The carton has a dozen compartments. Each compartment is a facet of your life: business, personal relationships, family life, hobbies, travel, financial matters, and the like. Now think of this egg carton smashed, with all of these facets running into one another. The more these facets touch one another, the more difficult it is to separate the issues when making a decision. It is very difficult to measure the amount of an important ingredient you need when it's part of a giant pool.

Let's take a closer look at how you see yourself. There's business, and then there's you, but often these lines get blurred. Are you the business? What would happen if you were not there? Have you built a team? How do you describe yourself to others? With whom do the important relationships reside?

Frequently, I hear an entrepreneur introduce herself as the company, as in, "Hi, Mary Smith, owner of Smith's Mattress Manufacturing and Distributing. You know, I'm the one in the commercials jumping up and down on the bed like I'm at a giant pajama party." While there's certainly nothing wrong with a little advertising, or even tooting your own horn a bit, it does make one wonder if there is any separation between Mary and the mattress company.

For the lifestyle maker, it is often the goal to have enough money to live comfortably, to increase community standing as a business leader, and to be involved in church and/or charity to give back. Certainly these are admirable aspirations that can be obtained with relative ease by any successful business owner.

For the empire builder, the goal is often all of the above, with an intangible extra: the desire to maximize all of the hard work, energy, and resources available. The empire builder is often seen standing right next to the lifestyle maker. The only difference is that empire builders know how to leverage contacts, resources, and skills to work their plan, and they use their best business efforts to advance the business ball.

Now that doesn't mean that empire builders are disingenuous. Just the opposite; they are very genuine about their business relationships. Their employees work for the company, not for them personally. These employees know they are at work to do a job to the best of their ability each and every day. The outside contacts in the business world are just that, business contacts, and each is evaluated in terms of what they can bring to the table for the company.

Is this a cold, hard, insensitive person? No. These are the same people you see out enjoying an evening with their families, relaxing on the ski slopes of Colorado with friends, and entertaining the board of a local favorite charity. They have managed to draw a line between their personal lives and the business, and empire builders are secure in it all.

If you can't draw the line, or your company is there just to support a lifestyle, you could be a lifestyle maker.

FACTOR NUMBER FOUR:
PERSONAL RELATIONSHIPS

This is always a tricky one, so I will do my best to explain the situation as it relates to business. There is no doubt that having a close relationship with a client or a business influencer is important. When I think about this, I am always reminded of the old sales story about the fish on the wall.

In this story, the salesman from New York can't seem to get any business from his client in Idaho. Every time they meet at a convention or trade show they have a great time and leave saying they can't wait to talk to one another, but nothing happens. Finally, out of desperation, the salesman flies to Idaho to see if there is something he can do to talk his client into more business. When he gets to the office he sees a giant fish on the wall. Being an avid fisherman himself, he comments on the fish and the fishing trip he is taking to Los Cabos. Eyes wide, the client says he's always wanted to do that. Seizing the moment, the salesman says, "Well, it's something I do every year with my top clients. It lets me relax and learn more about their businesses so I can service them better." The salesman invites the client on the trip, and when they return, the orders begin to flow in. Bribing a client? No.

These two people just found something they could relate to on a more personal level, and it helped them bond. The trip, however, was framed in the context that it was for people serious about doing business.

If you don't know how or can't network with a purpose to use your business relationships to achieve a business end, you could be a lifestyle maker.

FACTOR NUMBER FIVE: THE WORLD AROUND YOU

Understanding what is happening both in terms of the big picture and on a more microscopic level is crucial to your business.

Building a business starts with a passel of emotions—passion, ambition, a sense of accomplishment, a desire to create something special. But once you're off and running, the danger of letting emotions rule in the strategic world of business is a key flaw that inhibits many entrepreneurs from creating wealth and achieving true financial security. It's painful to watch these owners ride the business bell curve back down to its bottom— unable to let go at the right time, uncertain of how to bring it to the next level. Too much of an emotional investment can lead to poor decisions that impact the value and vitality of the company. In the end, there is nothing more heartbreaking for an entrepreneur than to look back on the golden opportunity for financial freedom and business growth that could have been.

The Bell Curve

After I conducted a workshop in New York City, an attendee came up to me and told me the kind of story I hate to hear:

"My business was doing $80 million in revenue when someone offered to buy it for $50 million in cash," she explained. "I turned down the offer because I was doing well, and I figured it would keep on going like this. But, there was more to it than that. I really felt like I had given my business a life. I was committed to doing good in the community, and I believed I was fulfilling that mission by taking care of all these people in my company. I had created a culture that I enjoyed and saw my employees as my family.

"What I failed to realize was that the bulk of my business was in telecom. When the market crashed, so did my business. I had to let go of many of the people I was trying to protect, and I didn't know what it was going to take to go to the next level. Today, I'm doing $20 million in revenue, and I have to figure out how to get back to $80 million."

As she was about to walk away, she commented wistfully, "Do you know the good I could've done with the $50 million?"

On the other hand, as I write this chapter, my good friend Paul has just sold his company for the second time, earning a tidy sum for himself on both deals. How did that happen?

When Paul started his own investment management firm, the timing couldn't have been better. Interest rates were coming down, 401(k)s were just coming into vogue, and more and more individuals were investing in mutual funds. In general, the economy was healthy, and the future was bright for financial services. Five years later, when approached by a large firm that was executing a roll-up strategy, he sold out. What did the future of his company look like then? Pretty good, but he had come to a crossroads. Did he want to build a boutique or build an empire? What Paul understood was that the business landscape of his industry was changing, and the divide between the small firms and the 800-pound gorillas was growing ever wider with the midsize companies ending up nowhere. Paul studied his options: continue to grow slowly and organically on his own in an increasingly competitive environment, or sell to someone who had the resources to help him execute his vision.

Because Paul thinks like the empire builder he is, he sold his company to a major player in the industry and cut himself a very nice deal to stay on and execute his vision. For the next five years, he continued to execute his growth strategy, tripling the client base and the assets he managed.

Then the unthinkable happened. The stock market bubble burst, followed by the 9/11 terrorist attacks. Suddenly, no one wanted to be invested in mutual funds, and the value of the company declined.

Understanding market cycles, Paul made an offer to buy his company back for a fraction of what he originally sold it for. The parent company was happy to negotiate because it was looking for ways to raise capital and keep its own share price afloat in tough times. Back on his own, Paul knew he needed capital to continue to execute his strategy, so he raised some debt and equity and stayed focused on growing. Eventually, the market turned and the cloud lifted over the economy. What did Paul do? He took advantage of the upturn to sell the company again for almost twice what he paid the former parent company.

What is the difference between these two tales? Both businesses had hardworking, smart, and ambitious owners, but one had an owner who kept his finger on the pulse of the world around him and made sure that when the timing was right, he was able to move quickly. There are some things about business that you'll never be able to control, and one of them is the pace of your opportunities.

FACTOR NUMBER SIX: MAKING DECISIONS

A prospective client, Karen, is one of those inspirational entrepreneurs who started with nothing and yet managed to grow a manufacturing company to $20 million in revenue almost overnight. A sudden demand for her products caused her business to take off in a serious way. Now, with a company value in excess of $50 million, she knows she needs to make a move, but which one? She doesn't want to make a wrong decision, and she is frantically busy running her existing contracts, servicing customers, and managing operations on a day-to-day basis.

She has come to the conclusion that, at this moment, she simply doesn't have time to grow. She's decided to wait until she has the time to do the legwork, gather all the information, and ponder all the options.

In my experience, she'll be waiting forever. By the time she does decide she is ready to do something, it will probably be too late.

I don't want to sound like the voice of impending danger, but there really is something to the saying "Strike while the iron is hot." There's a right time for the right action. But faced with the daunting task of identifying, evaluating, structuring, and "doing the deal," many business owners have a tendency to travel the riskiest road—which is to take no action at all.

The High Cost of Inaction

There are a lot of reasons that entrepreneurs suffer from inertia, all of them based in fear (fear of the unknown, fear of being tossed aside, fear of the company growing too big and losing that "family feel") and avoidance of a process perceived to be messy and stressful. It seems there's a comforting misconception that to maintain an enterprise at existing levels of growth is to play it safe and sane. The truth is, while you might stay in one place, market demands, competitive strategies, and economic trends—not to mention unforeseen events such as 9/11 and the war with Iraq—can place your company in a very different position in a relatively short period of time.

As an investment banker, one of the things I help clients explore is what the "cost of inaction" will be. In other words, if you don't do anything, what are the potential financial outcomes for your company?

A good example is a nurse staffing company I know, a successful company in what has been one of the decade's hottest growth industries.

Two years ago, at the height of the market, this particular company had $5 million in earnings and could have traded at ten times its EBITDA (earnings before interest, taxes, depreciation, and amortization), or $50 million. Yet, the owner, anxious and confused about how to propel her company forward, decided to continue building her business and "think things out." While she was considering her options, larger companies in the industry were busy gobbling up smaller companies and contributing to the trend of industry consolidation, a practice that tends to cause a drastic drop in trade value.

As a result, that same nurse staffing company's value went from $50 million to $20 million in just two short years. That's the cost of inaction. It's a heavy price to pay for sitting still.

YOU DON'T HAVE TO
GO IT ALONE

One option for the business owner who is motivated but not fully confident of getting all facets of the job done is to seek out an investment banking firm. Investment banking firms can be a disinterested third party whose job it is to provide strategic counsel, identify and explore opportunities, crunch numbers, and negotiate the deal. Such firms are partners, not service providers; they only take on clients they believe are marketable and poised for growth. They do charge a fee—a modest retainer and a percentage of the transaction—but generally, those that use their services find it to be well worthwhile.

Another option is to network within business organizations and learn from those who have already been there and done that. There also is no shortage of books and courses in this area. The bottom line is that you have to be willing to make a commitment to grow and take the first strategic steps toward moving your company to the next level.

It may seem scary, but the investment in time and effort is far outweighed by the financial, personal, and professional gains you can enjoy once the deal is done.

HONEST EVALUATION

Take some time to think about yourself and how you view and run your company. There are key differences between being a lifestyle maker versus an empire builder—some subtle, some not—as shown in Figure 1. 1.

The following characterize the mind-set of lifestyle makers:

- Enjoy the challenge of running a business
- Are successful in their own eyes
- Enjoy their positions in the community

- Have developed a certain lifestyle from the income their company is spinning off
- Tend to be unconcerned with external market factors
- Enjoy moving the company forward on their own time frame
- Often think of the company as a child they have birthed and are content with watching it grow
- Think of employees as family

The following characterize the mind-set of empire builders:

- Enjoy the challenge of running a business
- Have a matrix by which to measure success
- Keep their personal lives separate from the business
- Understand exactly what the value drivers are

THE END GAME

The end game is where you are when you finally cash out, and this is where the real differences between lifestyle makers and empire builders become strikingly apparent. Both lifestyle makers and empire builders have worked hard and lived comfortable lives. At the exit, though, one is going to be worth substantially more than the other (see Chapter 2).

The lifestyle maker who avoided the harder decisions won't be as profitable because increasing the bottom line wasn't a big motivator. Businesses tend to sell on multiples of earnings, and that is important to remember. Also, the life-

FIGURE 1.1 *Lifestyle Maker vs. Empire Builder*

Lifestyle Maker	Empire Builder
Typically started the company without a real plan in mind	Plans his/her work, works his/her plan
Owner is happy doing it his/her way	Acutely aware of the competition and the business landscape
Unconcerned with external environment	Understands exactly what needs to be done each and every day to create the most value for the company
Living quite comfortably, usually both monetarily and as an established member of the community	Leverages contacts and resources
No real exit strategy	Maintains a divide between business and emotion
People pleaser	Relies mostly on research and empirical evidence for decisions
Blurred lines between the person and the company	Understands it is just business
Relies mostly on instinct	Acutely aware of the competition and the business landscape

style maker may have missed certain opportunities for growth of which the empire builder has taken advantage. Ultimately, the lifestyle maker may not be able to sell the company, pay taxes, and live the lifestyle to which he or she has become accustomed.

For example, if your manufacturing business does $20 million in revenue and you've been earning $3 million per year in EBITDA while taking home an annual salary of $1 million, you're in great shape for now. But if you sold your business for three to four times EBITDA (businesses trade at multiples of earnings, as we'll discuss in Chapter 2), your business may be worth $9 to $12 million in today's market. As a lifestyle maker, you are living quite well off your salary and business profits, but have you created true wealth? Probably not. When you sell your company, you'll be lucky to pocket $5 or $6 million after all is said and done. If you could earn 10 percent per year, that's $500,000 to $600,000, a far cry from the annual salary of $1 million to which you were accustomed!

On the other hand, the empire builder, by virtue of growing the business as effectively as possible on a daily basis with the proper capitalization, can easily end up selling for ten times the amount the lifestyle maker was paid—if the game is played right (see Figure 1.2).

The book's purpose is to get you to think like an empire builder. It gives you the tools to shape a mind-set that can free you from costly errors and enable you to take advantage of an opportunity when it comes along. You'll learn how to create the opportunities you need to at any stage of your business. You need a plan and you need to know how to execute that plan. The following chapters detail the empire builder's mind-set—how the "big boys" think—in more detail.

FIGURE 1.2 *What Empire Builders Know*

What Empire Builders Know

1. An empire is better than a village; as a matter of fact, it's easier to run an empire

2. Network with a purpose

3. Determine your resources and use them

4. Capital makes execution easier

5. At the end of the day, it's just business

CHAPTER TWO

Valuation

NOBODY HAS AN
UGLY BABY

Of all the issues that get in the way of growing or selling a company, valuation tops the list. I like to use the phrase "no one has an ugly baby," because I have yet to meet a business owner who wasn't in love with her company. It's the same kind of starry-eyed love that new parents have for their infants, but it sometimes engenders a form of blindness about how difficult the path to growth and maturity will be. Entrepreneurs and business owners are, by nature, optimists, the kind of people who tend to see the glass half full. Every day they awaken to a world full of pie-in-the-sky possibilities and, like good parents, use their best efforts to make everything happen.

Professional investors and dealmakers—the very people you need to grow your business—are just the opposite; they tend to see the glass half empty. People who buy and sell companies for a living or are employing a serious acquisition strategy take nothing on faith in the way they value a company and what they are looking to get out of a transaction. They need to see facts, figures, numbers, and comparisons before they make a move.

Why are the two approaches so different? Like most things, it has to do with your point of view. If every morning you get up and think about all of the glorious possibilities that lay before you; how you are going to conquer the universe; and why your company, brand, people, strategy, or any other attributes are the best around, then it is unsettling when you must talk to investors who are interested only in how much money you are currently making and how long it will take your business to grow by multiples of some impossibly huge number.

Businesses, like children, need constant nurturing. No child grows up to fulfill his parents' dreams in the absence of constant and conscientious parenting. Similarly, no start-up business venture can possibly realize the potential its owner envisions without careful planning to take advantage of the many opportunities there are to invest in or buy out. An objective, clear-eyed assessment of how much your company is worth is the place to start. In this chapter and the one that follows, we'll look at how potential investors assess your company as they determine how much it's worth. Valuation has tangible aspects, but it also has an element of judgment and opinion. I call it the "science" and "art" of valuation.

DETERMINING YOUR COMPANY'S VALUATION: AN ART OR A SCIENCE?

Like most aspects of business, there is both a science and an art to making things work. Recognizing both the tangible and intangible aspects of a company is what understanding valuation is really about. Let's first look at three common, "scientific" ways—facts, figures, and comparisons—that the worth of companies is evaluated and see how these methods apply to your business. Later in the chapter we will examine where the science falls short; that is, where facts and figures don't tell the entire story of your company's potential.

THE SCIENTIFIC APPROACH: FACTS, FIGURES, AND COMPARISONS

Looking at the bare business basics, it is most common to employ one or more of the following methods to put a starting valuation on your company.

Cash Flow: Valuation's Key Component

Because ultimately the market will determine what your company is worth, it is important to understand which attributes the market will pay for, and which, though nice to have, won't really add to the bottom line. What really matters today is cash flow, cash flow, and more cash flow. You must have a repeatable, sustainable revenue model, and "Cash Is

King" should be your mantra when building your business. Nothing "dings" valuation more than when a company must renew its revenue stream every 6 to 12 months. Ideally, if you can work in advance to lengthen the contracts you have, make sure they remain in place if there is a change of control, and show that there are long-term relationships with existing clients, then you have an asset that will positively impact your company's valuation.

Comparable public companies. When we show clients the figures of comparable publicly traded companies, we almost always hear, "But that company is really not like us." And that's true in most cases. The chances of finding two perfectly identical companies are about the same as finding two identical unrelated people. What this exercise provides is a basis from which to extrapolate some quantifiable industry data. For example, if ten public companies are trading with EBITDA margins of 10 percent and you are at 5 percent, then you know you have some work to do. Are your margins low because you are restricted by volume, geography, or competitive environment? If the norm is 10 percent and you are at 17 percent, will this percentage change as you grow? If you can state confidently that you can keep that advantage or increase the margin, you may have a unique advantage and could command a premium on your valuation.

By comparing your company to publicly traded companies, you can look at the difference between the multiples of sales, earnings, and margins. These comparisons are handy ways to determine the starting point for proper valuation levels. Bear in mind that closely held or privately held companies may trade at lower multiples than public companies do.

This is called an *illiquidity discount*. An illiquidity discount is the difference between what a company is worth when it's publicly traded and when it's privately held.

Here's how I like to explain it: When you have a publicly traded company, there's a ready market for that company that you can look up on the stock exchange and you can trade shares. A closely held company does not have a ready market. You have to create a market for that company and it's also going to be smaller and much less additive, usually, when it gets folded into the acquiring company. You get *discounted* (valued less) for the fact that your investor needs to go out and find the market for your company.

Discounted cash flow (DCF) analysis. DCF is another tool that potential investors in your company may use to quantify an investment or buy-side opportunity. Using projections, this method analyzes the future free cash flow and then discounts it (most often using the weighted average cost of capital) to arrive at a present value. Remember the emphasis above on repeatable, sustainable revenue streams? Having true sustainable revenue streams—through customer contracts, licensing arrangements, franchise fees, or the like—can be very helpful in determining or defending your company's value. Typically this technique projects a company's earnings five to ten years into the future. These projections are returned to a present value figure by applying the time value of money and a discount rate for the associated risk. A terminal value is applied for an analysis of a "going concern" business. This method entails an intricate understanding of your company and the industry.

Keep in mind that there are many variations on what you can use for your cash flow and what you decide the discount rate should be. The most important point to remember is that the projections and discount rate must be credible—that is, you need to be able to defend it rationally and intelligently—otherwise the exercise holds no importance in the valuation process.

Comparable private and public company transactions. This technique allows your company to be compared to recent mergers and acquisitions that have occurred in the marketplace over the past year. Revenue and EBITDA multiples are found for these selected transactions, which are then analyzed to find a mean and median. The comparable transactions multiples are then compared with the multiples of your company and a potential trading multiple is derived.

■ REMEMBER

Multiples do not drive value. They are a way in which value can be expressed.

Again, it is important to realize that each transaction that occurs in the market has its own set of circumstances surrounding it.

These three ways of deriving a value for a given company—comparing it to publicly traded companies, running a DCF analysis, and recent comparable transactions—are what I think of as the "science" of valuation in selling a company, because unless you have developed the next cancer-curing drug or life-altering software, your business will be valued at current market prices. Why? Because the market is the great equalizer and when it comes to buying or investing in private companies, it will always speak the truth. You therefore need to understand what's going on in your business's market from the beginning. It is critical early on in your company's life cycle to understand how companies are valued so that when you decide to sell or merge, you will be in control of all the valuation factors and how they're applied. You always want to be in the driver's seat. Ignoring the factors that go into the valuation process will result in an inaccurate picture of your company and delay the building of your business empire and the achievement of your financial goals.

Other Empirical Evidence That Counts

Historical earnings. It is often said that the best time to sell your company is when you are on your way up. Buyers and investors don't like to fix other people's problems. They are looking for situations that enhance the value of their own companies or can be grown easily with an infusion of capital. It's a good idea to begin thinking about your exit from your business almost from day one and work hard to make sure that your earnings always show a nice upward trajectory, that your margins are within or exceeding industry standards, and that last year's good results were not just a "one-hit wonder" but demonstrate the company's ability to generate a nice growth rate year after year.

Customer diversity. Who are your top 20 clients or customers? Does any one customer make up a disproportionate amount of your revenue? Think about your customer base not only by name but also by industry. Industries that are cyclical in nature (for example, telecom, housing, and energy) can cause you to have choppy earnings based on their industry cycles, not yours. Government contracts can easily fall into this category, too. If you are selling into programs favored by a particular administration or someone's pet project, you could wake one day to find a new administration that is looking to cut back its spending in the middle of your project.

■ REMEMBER

To increase valuation, make customer diversity an asset of your company. If you have too many eggs in one basket, you will be as vulnerable as your customers to the changing dynamics and pricing pressures of their sector. Be mindful of the bubbles and make sure you are insulated from boom-bust cycles.

Size. Size is always one of the toughest issues with which business owners grapple. There is no doubt that the bigger the company, the stronger the multiple it will receive on its earnings. The dilemma is how big any one individual can realistically grow the company on her own. A company with $10 million in revenue is much more attractive to potential investors than one with $1 to $5 million; $25 million beats $10 million; $50 million beats $25 million; $100 million beats $50 million; and so on. Why? If a company is truly scalable, then the economics should be increasing and dropping substantially more earnings to the bottom line as the company gets bigger.

The larger the company, the more opportunity it presents to the buyer or investor too. Remember, the investor or acquirer works just as hard trying to complete a deal that will grow your company by $5 million as he or she does on another deal that could add $50 million in revenue earnings to his or her top line, or $5 million in revenue to the bottom line.

Often it is worth your while to sweat out a few more years and reach that bigger revenue and earning target before seeking out investors or buyers, because your valuation is based on the multiples, not just the earnings. See "The Power of Size on Multiple Expansion" for an example.

■ REMEMBER

Ask yourself if it's worth the wait to get to a more meaningful size before thinking about recapitalizing or exiting.

Niche markets. Niches can be great selling points as long as they are true—not bogus—markets, meaning they have a feature that is unique in the marketplace; for instance, a computer technology company whose software addresses the specific needs of state and local governments, or a medical supply company that has developed a product that focuses on the issue of memory loss within the aging population. Buyers look for situations where it will be easier to grow through an acquisition than to build a company themselves and very often will pay handsomely for the convenience. This rule applies in products, services, and geogra-

THE POWER OF SIZE ON MULTIPLE EXPANSION

Abby Co., an industrial manufacturer of wire and piping for fences, kennels, and corrals, earns $36 million in revenues annually, and earns $4 million of EBITDA. We know from looking at comparable companies and market transactions that companies of this type and size generally trade in a range of multiples from three to five times EBITDA. So this company would be worth $12 to $20 million.

Recent transactions in this type of manufacturing industry show us that similar companies with revenues over $50 million trade at multiples of five to seven times earnings, meaning that if Abby Co. can increase its revenue from $36 to $50 million and grow its pretax earnings from $4 to $6 million, it would then trade between $30 and $42 million—a substantial premium to the smaller, more illiquid company.

One of the reasons for this valuation is because at $50 million in revenue, the company becomes a much more meaningful player in the market: It is better able to attract capital to help fuel its growth and is of a size that is more attractive to potential acquirers. (More on this phenomenon in Chapter 7.)

phy. For instance, a company that is producing garden fountains may decide that its clients are also looking for other items to enhance gardens and patios. It may be easier to purchase a company that specializes in outdoor furniture and garden ornaments, rather than start up a new division, so that they can quickly use their existing sales channels to drive more products to their customer base. The FedEx-Kinko's merger is a recent example of a situation where two niche companies came together to bundle client services. It is very common to see companies acquire a mom-and-pop operation that "owns" a particular geography rather than to try to build a geographic presence by competing with the hometown favorite.

■ REMEMBER

Companies with products or advantages that are attractive to larger companies looking to expand get paid a higher valuation.

Proprietary products and business process. Do you own any intellectual property that makes your company stronger than competitors? If so, are patents, trademarks, and copyrights all in good order? Recently, a venture capitalist friend of mine told the story of a company his firm was trying to buy that has several dozen patents. In the course of due diligence, they discovered that while the patents had been issued, they were filed for incorrectly. The company had filed as a small corporation instead of a larger entity and the patents were therefore invalid! You can imagine how much that impacted the company's valuation.

When evaluating what sets your company apart, don't forget your business processes. Think about what a firm like McKinsey & Company does. This giant consultancy has forged a global empire based on the methods it employs in the course of working with its clients. It has developed tools, templates, and models that have proven highly successful in helping clients solve problems and evaluate strategy. These business processes add significant value to its organization and set it apart as the gold standard of the consulting world.

■ REMEMBER

Your business may have some of these proprietary products or processes too. Proper documentation will significantly impact valuation.

THE DOWNSIDE OF VALUATION: WHAT GETS IN THE WAY

Your brand is bigger than your company. When   I come upon this situation, I am reminded of the Henry David Thoreau quote: "Do not worry if you have built your castles in the air; now put the foundations under them." Most often this situation arises in companies that have a product or service that has really grabbed the attention of the public and, more often than not, the media. While publicity is a great thing when building a brand, you need to remember that what really matters when evaluating your company is earnings. I recently was involved in a deal for someone who owned a high-end clothing brand. This brand had a huge presence in the media and the name was licensed by one of the of the big box retailers. But when we did an analysis of the financials, we saw that the brand was much bigger than what the revenue and earnings of that company actually reflected. This company had built castles in the air. The business attracted huge attention from major backers, but when they came in and looked at how little the business earned, the potential backers lost interest because the company did not have a solid financial foundation or the necessary infrastructure to support its scale. We will revisit this company when we look at SWOT analyses in Chapter 3.

The second part of Thoreau's quote speaks to what professional investors (private equity and venture capitalists) often do. Currently, we see a large number of brands being purchased by backers who will put the management teams, manufacturing facilities, systems, and capital behind them to create true value. Recent examples would be Burberry, Lilly Pulitzer, and Jane Cosmetics. For all of these companies, investors recognized that the brand was more valuable than the company, and set about to put each entity on a more solid financial footing. You can do this organically too if you understand how to put a solid foundation underneath a brand. Take the example of the trendy women's wear brand Tory Burch, which started out as a small brand and is now in many major department stores throughout the country. She built her business in a very smart way. Starting in New York City, she then opened stores in Los Angeles, Atlanta, and Dallas. If she decides to go to the capital markets, she can truthfully claim that her merchandise sells in Bergdorf's and Saks, but it also sells in Phipps Plaza in Atlanta and Highland Park Village in Dallas. She knows that people are buying items online, so she can make the claim that her brand has national appeal. She proved beyond a doubt she is a national brand and not a boutique label, and now has the empirical evidence to convince potential investors or buyers of this fact.

You are the company. While we all like to see our name in lights, there's something to be said for *not* reading your own press.

Many entrepreneurs and business owners are fantastic marketers, able to gather hordes of publicity about themselves. Certainly no one can argue that being quoted in trade journals and winning industry awards are good things, but you must be able to point out conclusively that this flurry of attention is about the company and not you. Otherwise you will have created a situation that, without you, the business has little value.

■ REMEMBER

Nothing deflates valuation like a star owner whose company is solely dependent on that person's personality, flair, and contacts.

Revenues you don't control. In today's business environment, it is common practice for large companies to outsource to second-tier vendors or strike licensing agreements for use of a name. While this is a fantastic opportunity to do business with the big boys, it is not valued the same way it would be if you controlled the account yourself. There is a risk to a buyer or financing source that an outside circumstance could harm the primary relationship. Because the purchasing decision lies with the first-tier supplier, your revenues could be adversely affected.

For example, if you have a licensing agreement with a company and your revenue relies heavily on the licensee's ability to market and sell your product, then you are not in control of that revenue stream, and your valuation will be impacted by the risk of this arrangement.

Concentration issues. Just as a third-party relationship can be debilitating to valuation, having too many eggs in one basket can also ding valuation. Too much revenue with any one customer, too many important relationships with one salesperson, too much reliance on one supplier or vendor, or too large a percentage of sales in a particular geographic area are concentration issues that can negatively affect valuation.

If you license your name, product, or technology to a single distributor where there are "hooks" in the agreement that prohibit you from doing business with the distributor's competition, those hooks can cause concentration issues. The arrangement may go so far as to limit who else in a given territory or market sector you can sell your products through. Concentration of talent, customers, or your revenue stream is something that hurts valuation. Concentration could be any one of the following aspects of valuing a company:

- You *are* the company, as discussed above.
- You have too few customers; for example, 50 percent of your business is with three clients.

- You have too few sources of required materials to run your business; you would be sunk if you lose *one* of your sources.
- You have too many relationships tied up with one particular person in that company. If you lose that person, you lose multiple relationships and your company is in trouble.

The point is: Concentration can kill valuation. An obvious example would be a chip manufacturer such as Intel relying on three customers—for instance, Dell, IBM, and Apple. One day, if Apple announces that it will make its own computer chip, or will seek a competing supplier for its chip, Intel would have a very big problem because it will lose one-third of its customer base. The point is that if you only have a few places where you are going with your goods or services, you are very vulnerable and that vulnerability affects valuation because your company is at risk.

OTHER FACTORS IN THE VALUATION EQUATION

Below is a list of other factors that may influence the valuation of your company:

- Amount of revenue you generate
- Your customer concentration

- Operating history
- Amount of debt your have taken on
- Market saturation
- Market position
- Depth of your management

Most of these factors are self-evident. What the investor or buyer is doing by coming up with a valuation is to place a number on the company that he or she can live with, given the risks associated with the transaction.

But I want to emphasize that solid financial controls in valuing a company are very important. Solid financial controls are what make a company worth *more*.

VALUATION THROUGH THE BUYER'S OR INVESTOR'S EYES

All that buyers are doing when they are evaluating a company for purchase is assessing the price they are paying versus the risk they are taking.

Every time potential buyers uncover something they believe is a risk to the business they are investigating, the risk bell goes off in their heads and they lower the valuation of that company. It's a *very simple* equation.

THE INTANGIBLE EXTRAS: WHAT ELSE MAKES YOUR BUSINESS WORTH MORE

The "intangible extras" of company value are the factors beyond both the numbers and the "art" that can influence the value of your company. For instance, when you sell a house, you make sure that it is clean, well lit, and in good repair before putting it on the market. Any records of replacement work done—fixing the roof, installing a new air-conditioning system, cleaning the water heater—can enhance the value. Similarly, there are also certain intangibles that can augment the value of your business. Having all of the books, records, and contracts together and presenting the data in a way that a prospective buyer or investor could readily use, for instance, will enhance the overall impression one has of you and your company.

Financial statements. It cannot be emphasized enough: Prepare your company early by getting its financial house in order. Accurate accounting statements are truly a place where you don't want to be penny-wise and pound-foolish. Financial statements should be audited by a reputable firm. No lender, investor, or buyer is going to take a bookkeeper's word when it comes to reconciliation of the numbers; often a transaction will get held up while an audit is completed.

Budgets and projections should be clearly outlined, reviewed, and constantly honed to reflect the true state of the market. Strong internal controls, reviews, and procedures send a clear message that you run a tight ship, understand what is going on in your company, and demonstrate an air of professionalism.

An immediate benefit is that by taking a complete look at your numbers, you will get a much better idea of what is working and why. With this information, you can fix issues in a timely manner that are costing you valuable dollars and could ultimately hurt your valuation.

I can think of several instances when, during the due diligence process, a company was not able to come up with accurate documentation to support revenues.

One example was a subscription-based company that could not quickly provide documentation on its client base. When asked by the buyer for such data as the number of renewals each year, the number of new clients, and the system for tracking subscribers, the company came up blank. We knew that they had solid numbers because they had revenues from their subscribers' credit card charges, but without understanding how many customers were renewals and how many were new, there was no way to quantify this company's cost of customer acquisition.

Management. This is the one area that is make or break when it comes to evaluating a company, because having the right management in place shows up in everything the company does—from reputation to business process, from vision to execution. If your company does not have an A+ team, don't expect an A+ price.

Do you have the team on board to take you where you want to go? You may sell your company to a buyer who doesn't care about the management team, but for the most part when people look to invest in a company, they are investing in the management. If they are acquiring the company, the chances are they're going to keep that management, at least for a while. And often they are simply looking to acquire talent. That would be a reason to buy a company. Very solid management bodes well for the valuation of the entire transaction.

Barriers to entry. This is a very important consideration when valuing a company. Traditionally we think of patents, trademarks, licenses, etc., as the important items affecting barrier to entry. Other barriers could be a fierce competitive environment that limits growth and lack of talent to carry forth the company's goals.

Product and sales pipeline. Can you define on paper for your prospective buyer or investor how the future for your business looks and why? Padding a sales projection with a bunch of bogus numbers will look like just that—padding. Take the time now to shore up your sales and make sure you will hit your projections as you move through the transaction process.

Written plans, policies, and procedures. The more you can demonstrate that nothing happens by chance, the better you will look to an outside set of eyes. As the saying goes, "What gets measured gets met."

Goodwill. Goodwill is often used to describe the value of a company over and above its tangible assets. Factors that play into goodwill are customer loyalty, reputation, name recognition, and the number of years you've been in business.

Black's Law Dictionary defines goodwill as "the ability of a business to generate income in excess of a normal rate on assets due to superior managerial skills, market position, new product technology and so on." If you follow the guidelines, you can set the gold standard in your industry and command a premium.

Other assets. Customer lists, trademarks, and proprietary databases are the secret sauce. Any information or material you have acquired that is not publicly available and gives your company an extra edge in the marketplace can be considered very valuable to the company's valuation.

Understanding how a business is valued will keep you out of the weeds. In other words, by constantly striving to achieve the highest valuation for your company, you will be less likely to take on low-margin business, allow too little customer diversity, and retain employees who no longer add value to the company. You will also be in a better position to evaluate risk because you will understand the payoff on the back end. In short, you will approach your company as your largest portfolio holding and expect it to deliver maximum market performance. Like a proud parent, you will reap rewards that make the effort of nurturing and growing your business an extremely satisfying endeavor.

What Negatively Affects Valuation	What Positively Affects Valuation
Inconsistent or lumpy earnings (that lead to poor operating results)	Strong management team
Weak or declining margins	Recurring and renewable revenue stream
Revenue growth that is sub-par in the industry	Differentiated products/brand recognition
Customer, supplier, or vendor concentration	Premium pricing for products
Pent-up capital expenditures	Patents and proprietary processes
Debt on the balance sheet	High barrier to entry
Probability of product or technology obsolescence	Loyal customer base

Valuation—Seller Issues

- It's not what you receive for your business
- It's not how much tax you pay
- It's what you can earn (after tax) from the proceeds of the business
- Early planning minimizes taxes and optimizes after-tax earnings

Chapter 3 is very closely related to this one and is important for you to understand as you grow your business to the next level.

CHAPTER THREE

Growing Strategically, Growing Smart

When I meet with owners of closely held companies, one of the first questions I ask is, How are you going to grow your business? Almost universally the answer is "organically." In this chapter, I outline alternative growth strategies used by high-growth companies that are available to you. Once you have decided to become an empire builder and have taken off the rose-colored glasses through which you previously viewed your company's worth and style, you are set to face fact number one: In business, if you are not growing, you're dying.

Why? Because while you may be quite comfortable with where your business is, there is a competitor out there practicing the basic business principles I am outlining in this book. That competitor is positioning itself to grab your market share and, in the process, eliminate you, its competition!

Now that you understand the issue of valuation, you will be able to make better, faster, and more strategic decisions that will ultimately fuel your company's growth.

Let me be clear: I am not advocating that every business launch into a wild merger and acquisition strategy. I am, however, suggesting that you develop a plan for understanding how you should grow that includes a way to keep your opportunities in sight. My former business partner, Hugh McColl, the erstwhile chairman of Bank of America who grew Nations Bank through more than 100 acquisitions into one of the world's largest consumer banks, always said, "You can't control the pace of your opportunities." If that's true—and I believe it is—then the best thing you can do is to be prepared to act fast if an opportunity appears.

SWOT ANALYSIS

Many entrepreneurs wouldn't know a business opportunity if it reached out and bit them! Vital to evaluating an opportunity to grow is to know your business, your competitors, and your industry inside and out using a SWOT analysis. SWOT is an acronym that stands for strengths, weaknesses, opportunities, and threats (see Figure 3.1).

Use the SWOT chart as a tool to get an honest evaluation of your business. This exercise is vital to developing a solid growth strategy.

SWOT analysis is a good way for you to evaluate your company's wherewithal. If you are thinking about growing or selling your company, bringing on capital, or going to the bank to get a loan, a SWOT chart is something you should complete up front. With it you can look at your company both

FIGURE 3.1 *SWOT Analysis Chart*

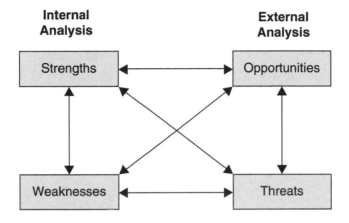

internally and externally, meaning that you can evaluate your company and then, with an external SWOT, consider:

- What's going on in your industry?
- What's not going on in your industry?
- What's going on with your competitors?

A SWOT analysis can help you answer these questions. All too often we look only at what is going on inside our organization and miss the bigger picture: A trend or a shift in market dynamics that could signal opportunity and a need to shift priorities.

The other thing to keep in mind when doing a SWOT analysis is that there are lots of factors, such as regulatory issues and global competition, that can affect your decisions as you consider growing your company. Depending on your industry, these issues need to be on your radar screen sooner rather than later. You cannot live like an ostrich in today's global economy.

Strengths

Strengths are skills, capabilities, and core competencies that help you achieve your goals and objectives. The list of your company's strengths should include what you do better than your competition and why. Also, think about how your competition sees you. Those areas could also be considered your company's strengths.

Strengths can include:

- Management team
- Recurring revenue
- Differentiated product
- Premium pricing
- Low-cost production
- Patents/proprietary processes
- Customer relationships
- Proprietary software/equipment

Ask and answer the following questions:

- What advantages does my company have?
- What do we do better than anyone else?
- What unique or lowest-cost resources do we have access to?
- What do people in our market see as our strengths?

Here are specific examples of what a company's strengths might be:

- We are able to respond very quickly because we have no red tape, no need for higher management approval, etc.
- We are able to give good customer care because our current level of work flow means we have plenty of time to devote to customers.
- Our lead salesperson has a strong reputation within the market.
- We are nimble and can change direction quickly if we find that our marketing is not working.
- We have little overhead, so we can offer pricing breaks to customers.

Consider strengths from an internal perspective *and* from the point of view of your customers and people in your market. Be realistic; it's far too easy to fall prey to the "this is the way it's done" syndrome without really thinking through what sort of impact a process or best practice may have. If you are having any difficulty describing your strengths, try making a list of your company's characteristics. Some of these will hopefully be strengths.

Also look at your strengths in relation to your competitors. For example, if all your competitors provide high-quality products, then providing high-quality products is not a strength in the marketplace. It is a competitive norm.

Weaknesses

Weaknesses are areas in which your business does not shine or stand out, or where there are concerns in your business model. Some of the weaknesses that you might need to address in order to grow your business include:

- Owner dependence
- Customer concentration
- Commodity products
- Lack of financial controls
- Concentrated sourcing
- One source of supply
- Lack of capital
- Unions
- Existing legal issues

Some questions you could ask yourself are:

- What could we improve?
- What should we avoid?
- Do we have the right people?
- What are people in our market likely to see as weaknesses?

Again, consider weaknesses from an internal *and* external point of view. Do other people seem to perceive weaknesses that you do not see? Are your competitors doing any better in a particular area than you are? It is best to be realistic now, and face any unpleasant truths as soon as possible, so you can create opportunities to correct them.

Specific examples of a company's weaknesses might be:

- Our company has no market presence or reputation.
- We have a small staff with a shallow skills base in many areas.
- We are vulnerable to vital staff illness, turnover, etc.
- Our cash flow will be unreliable in the early stages.
- I am this business. Without me, it would not function.
- Our products are seasonal, making cash flow unpredictable.

What to do about weaknesses. If your company does not have a critical skill or capability that it needs to achieve a particular goal, you have three choices:

1. Modify the goal to something you can achieve with the resources (time, people, money) you currently have (growth limiting)
2. Raise capital and acquire the skill or capability you need (growth enhancing)
3. Find another company that has the piece you are missing and either acquire it or form a strategic alliance (growth enhancing)

Opportunities

Opportunities are areas into which your business might expand or improve. These areas are remarkably similar to weaknesses. It just depends on your point of view. Some obvious business opportunities include:

- New trends in the marketplace
- Technology advances that aid your business model
- Changes in demographic profiles that enhance your market
- Changes in government regulations that favor your business

But they can also include:

- Owner dependence
- Customer concentration
- Commodity products
- Lack of financial controls
- Concentrated sourcing
- One source of supply
- Lack of capital
- Unions
- Existing legal issues

Useful opportunities also can come from such things as:

- Changes in technology and markets on both a broad and narrow scale
- Changes in government policy related to your field
- Changes in demographic and psychographic profiles
- Market events

Questions to ask yourself about opportunities for business growth are:

- Where are the good opportunities facing us?
- What are the interesting industry trends of which we are aware?

- How can we run with this new technology to increase sales/customer contact, etc.?
- What information would I like to extract from my lunch with Competitor A next week?

Specific examples of a company's opportunities might include:

- An expanding business sector, with many new possibilities for success
- A civic council that wants to encourage local businesses with work where possible
- Competitors who may be slow to adopt new technologies while your IT person is on top of innovations

A useful approach when looking at opportunities is to consider your strengths and ask yourself whether these open up any opportunities.

Alternatively, look at your weaknesses and ask yourself whether you have any opportunities to eliminate them.

Threats

Threats are areas in which your business is vulnerable to attack from outside forces that may or may not be under your control. With threats, knowledge about their existence and how to deal with them is vital to the growth of your business.

Threats to the growth of your business might include:

- Current competitors
- Foreign competitors
- Regulatory and legal environment
- Competitive products
- Substitute products
- Macroeconomic factors (e.g., rising fuel costs, interest rates, etc.)

Some questions to ask yourself as you evaluate threats to growing your business are:

- What obstacles do we face?
- What is our competition doing?
- Are the required specifications for our jobs, products, or services changing?
- Is changing technology threatening our position?
- Do we have bad debt or cash-flow problems?
- Could any of our weaknesses seriously threaten our business?

Carrying out this analysis will be an eye-opening experience because you will see what needs to be done, and whether or not your obstacles are as large or small as you perceive. In other words, you will get some perspective on which to base future decisions about growth plans.

Some specific examples of threats to a company might be:

- Developments in technology could change the market beyond our ability to adapt.
- A small change in the focus of a large competitor could wipe out any market position we achieve.
- We must deal with the fact that our product is being made in another country for a fraction of what it would cost to make it here.
- Rising fuel costs could threaten our competitive advantage.

After studying your business's threats, you may decide to specialize in rapid response and good value services to local businesses. Marketing would be in selected local publications to get the greatest possible market presence for a set advertising budget. You will need to keep up to date with changes in technology where possible.

ANALYZING THE ANALYSIS

One thing that's very interesting about a SWOT analysis is that weaknesses can be the same as opportunities. The reason the chart (shown in Figure 3.1) is formatted this way is that sometimes your strengths also are your weaknesses. Opportunities can be threats. Strengths can equal opportunities. Opportunities can point out weaknesses. Strengths can point out threats.

Once you've completed the SWOT analysis of your own company (an internal SWOT), do one for your industry and competitors (an external SWOT). For example, let's say one of your company's strengths is a state-of-the-art manufacturing facility. The only problem is that it's in New Jersey. The reason this is a problem is because most of your competitors have state-of-the-art manufacturing facilities in China and are manufacturing the same products at one-third your unit costs. This presents an opportunity because you can advertise that your product is made in the United States, you are supporting workers at home, and so forth. But it also can be a threat because your competition can come into the market-place and undercut you on prices. On the other hand, you have the opportunity to go overseas and manufacture part of your goods at a lower cost to remain competitive. As you can see, there are many different ways to analyze a threat and turn it into an opportunity—but you can only do this if you know what that threat is and prepare a plan of action.

I looked at a company recently that does debt collection for big banks and credit card companies. This company's business is booming, but a recent change in the industry may have some effect on its operations. MBNA was bought by Bank of America, which will consolidate the debt collection activities of both companies. Bank of America is not one of this debt collection company's customers, so the company needs to do a SWOT analysis to determine what impact this industry change will have on its business.

Let's look at the clothing retailer I mentioned in Chapter 2, the one whose brand was well known but had built castles in the air. The company did not have

- good financial controls,
- a solid management team,

- good business practices in place, or
- strength in its sourcing and manufacturing components.

In creating a SWOT analysis of this company, these defi-
ciencies would be illustrated as weaknesses. The only over-
arching strengths the company had were the creativity of the
founder and CEO and the big brand name. The rest of the
company's characteristics fell into the weaknesses side of the
SWOT chart.

As a result, the threats to this company were enormous.

- There was no barrier to entry and the market was
  quickly getting saturated.
- An aggressive competitor was in the middle of a major
  national expansion, including opening a flagship store
  on Madison Avenue in New York City—retail's mecca.
- There was no geographic diversity—all locations were
  in and around New York City. (No, it's not about marketing, what we are speaking to is that you need to
  prove that your company will play in New York City as
  well as in Peoria.

This big-brand company had *not* proven that outside the
tri-state area, women would actually spend *up* to buy expensive trendy casual clothes, whereas its competitor (which is a
publicly traded company, by the way) was in the process of
honing its brand nationally and had opened stores in select
spots nationwide that were doing well. Quite frankly, during
the time we had the deal in the market, the competitor's pub-

licly traded stock rose from $7 per share to $23 per share. It absolutely exploded.

Like the owner of this company, you may not even be aware of how weak (or strong) the foundation of your company is until you do a SWOT analysis.

SWOT Your Competitors

A SWOT analysis is a framework for analyzing your company's strengths and weaknesses, and the opportunities and threats you face. You can also apply a SWOT analysis of your competitors. As you do this, you'll start to see how and where they come up short and how your company can compete against them.

Evaluating your competitors will also help you to focus on your strengths, minimize weaknesses, and take the greatest possible advantage of opportunities available.

BUILD VERSUS BUY

You often hear businesspeople talking about "build versus buy." It's a catchphrase for the decision every entrepreneur must make about the best and most strategic ways to grow a business. Lifestyle makers prefer to grow their businesses "organically," meaning to build them from the foundation up. What they need to consider is growing their businesses through strategic acquisitions, the way empire builders would. What goes into a strategic acquisition plan that leads to growth?

There are many different ways to grow your business:

- Organic growth
- Merger and acquisition (M&A)
- Outside capital
- Strategic partnerships and alliances
- Franchising licensing

First, let's look at the strategic drivers of company growth that might lead to an M&A situation. I am not advocating wildly running down the M&A trail. However, I do feel that it is a very important growth strategy and one that should not be overlooked or minimized.

Using the chart in Figure 3.2, you can evaluate what can be achieved best through organic growth and where a good strategic acquisition strategy might make more sense in achieving your growth objectives.

Competition

As the saying goes, "Keep your friends close and your enemies closer." It never hurts to have a speaking relationship with other CEOs in your industry. Believe me, the heads of megacorporations do this all the time. That's why private clubs exist and there is so much controversy surrounding those that don't admit women as members!

FIGURE 3.2 *Strategic Drivers of Merger and Acquisition*

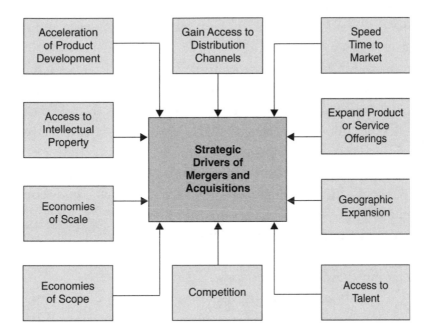

You want to know what your competition is doing all the time. Try to think of it this way. You never know if the CEO of your closest competitor is looking to sell. These executives may not even know they are thinking of selling in the near future when they tell you about the retirement home they purchased at the beach or reveal that their wife really wants to move to the opposite coast to be closer to the grandchildren. Many times smart deals happen because you are in the right place at the right time, so don't be afraid to position yourself among the ones you admire and respect the most in your industry.

An ancillary benefit to your recognizance is that your competitors will likely be good sources of other industry tidbits that could prove useful to your SWOT analysis. Which companies are not doing so well? Which ones are having management, customer, or supplier issues? Issues such as these will arise in casual conversations. If you can keep all of this information filed and organized in a user-friendly fashion, you will be in a great position to better evaluate an acquisition opportunity should it appear before you. Better yet, you might be able to make that opportunity happen.

What other information can you learn? Maybe your competition wants to buy your company and you had no idea they were in a financial position to do so. Maybe there is someone who is working for your competitor who might be interested in coming over the fence to work for you.

You can get a lot of information from your competition. There's nothing wrong with being friendly competitors. That's really how they do it in big business and you have to remember that even if you are not watching the competition, they certainly are watching you! So you might as well get in that game.

Growth Strategies

Geographic expansion. This is an area of which, in terms of selling or growing a business, you want to be mindful. Where are your geographic opportunities? What companies are in areas where you would like your products and services to be? For example, suppose you are on the East Coast and there is a great company you could acquire on the West Coast that would know just how to distribute your product. Wouldn't it be a lot easier to acquire its facilities and its people who already know the ropes than to go out and try to expand into that market from scratch? Geographic expansion includes international expansion as well, and is something of which to be mindful. During the time that I have been writing this book, the way business views geographic expansion has changed dramatically. Traditionally, entrepreneurs would look at geographic expansion on a north, south, east, and west basis within their own country. Of course, with the rise of Internet retailing, all this has changed. Rather than expand geographically, you might need to expand your company's Web site—but only if you are ready to handle all the increased business.

Expanding product or service offerings. Every time you leave a meeting or a sales call, isn't there one product or service you wish you offered that you could have sold to that account? When you consider build versus buy, I encourage you to think big. Think like the big players do. Get a white board in your office and start to list all the products and services you wish you could offer to your customers that you don't currently offer. Study the list, then think about whether there is another company you could acquire or that could acquire you to accomplish this same goal. If you had capital, could you go after an acquisition that would expand your product or service offerings in exactly the way you want to?

When you examine your customer base, do you find that there are products or services that easily complement what you currently offer? If so, then you should begin to look at which offerings can be acquired and which make more sense to build out internally.

■ REMEMBER

Even if it is not a core competency now, buying the right complement can give you a real advantage over your competition. For example, if you are a company that provides health care transportation and ambulance services and you hear repeatedly that one of the biggest issues in the 911 market is language translation, then a logistics and transportation company might be a perfect fit. Another example is a garden supply manufacturer that also is considering offering a line of patio furniture—items that the supplier knows its customers would be interested in purchasing. What makes more sense? Acquiring a company and brand already established in the space, or trying to build it out?

Time and speed to market. This is another aspect of the build-or-buy decision you need to consider. Often, if you need to get something in the market quickly, acquiring it is faster than building it from the ground up. The gardening supply manufacturer that wishes to sell outdoor furniture could do so more quickly by acquiring a patio furniture manufacturer rather than attempting to manufacture the furniture itself.

Time and speed to market are among many factors to consider when making a build-or-buy decision. Is there a time factor? If so, what is the opportunity cost if you don't act quickly? If your evaluation determines there isn't an opportunity cost your build-or-buy decision must rely on factors other than time.

Gaining access to distribution channels. This is an interesting area today because we have so many different distribution channels. For instance, in addition to customers walking into a brick-and-mortar store, a retailer can market its products on the Internet, through television outlets such as QVC, or by direct marketing through catalogs. People share, combine, and buy mailing lists all the time. There are fulfillment centers to assist companies with distribution. There are dozens of ways for a company to touch consumers. So ask yourself, what types of retail outlets do I need to drive my products into the marketplace that I don't already have and who has them?

Acceleration of product development. As mentioned above, in build-or-buy decisions, speed to market is sometimes of the essence. Drug companies make this assessment all the time. When they want to manufacture a drug that cures a specific illness or relieves certain symptoms, they know it would be much faster to acquire smaller companies that have already developed that drug rather than trying to develop the drug in house. Their goal is to get the product into the marketplace before their competitors so they can reap the benefits of being first to market.

Another example of this would be a drug company that has an established over-the-counter medication that consumers would like in a time-released version. Through industry analysis, this company learned that a competitor has developed a similar time-released medication that it is about to bring to market. To remain competitive in this market, it might be faster to acquire a company that already has developed the time-release technology rather than assigning its own research scientists to conduct the development and test the process. Without accelerating the product development process, this company risks losing market share to its competitor.

Access to intellectual property. There was a time in the go-go days of the 1990s when a patent could realize a huge windfall for a company—an automatic $100 million, let's say. While that might be a bit of an exaggeration, it was a crazy, frenzied time. Today things are very different and I often tell people that a patent is only as good as your pockets are deep to defend it. It's scary, and you also have to be aware of obsolescence.

Sometimes the scenario is a bit different: the infringing company, in this case Company A, will make a low-ball offer to buy the patented process knowing that eventually it will be obsolete. Company B doesn't have any choice but to accept the offer because it too is aware of the obsolescence factor and it doesn't have the financial wherewithal to take the process to the next level.

When you think about the advantage you have with a proprietary property, consider how strong it really is. How strong are the barriers to entry into the marketplace? High-tech service firms are recent casualties of easy access to a marketplace that changed and consolidated with almost breathless speed. However, this is not always the case. If you have the next widget that is the be-all and end-all of widgets and you can sustain it in the marketplace, you can command a very high price for its patent.

Acquiring or merging with a company that triples your business, quadruples your volume, and places you in a competitive advantage for the foreseeable future always makes perfect sense. Your costs for raw materials may go down, and you may have more goods or services that you can drive though your pipelines (distribution channels).

Access to talent/management. In the current business climate, you can't survive without a top management team in place. In the M&A game, it's all about talent and management. If this piece is residing someplace else, in some other company or sector, you have to go get it.

Now that we have covered the elements that go into build-or-buy decisions, it's also helpful to consider your potential investors' point of view.

EVALUATING THE TRANSACTION: WHAT ARE THE FINANCIAL ACQUIRERS SEEKING?

As we learned in Chapter 2, valuation of your company is both an objective and subjective process. The players, that is, the investors in or buyers of your company, will want to see repeatable, sustainable revenues. They are looking for a rate of return (IRR), a solid management team, and other more subjective factors that will make the acquisition immediately additive, such as those that follow.

Long-term trends in your industry. Strategic players know that the time to sell a business is when the company is on an upward trajectory, not when it's turned a corner and is on its way down or perhaps missed an opportunity to grow.

What are the long-term prospects for your company in its industry? If the business was started 20 years ago and it's taken 20 years to go from $5 million to $45 million in revenues, what do you expect that business to do in the next seven years, particularly if there is another down cycle? Are you going to be able to grow the value of your company enough to justify not doing something right now to take advantage of a booming M&A market?

Your business plan versus reality. If you are interested in selling your company, your potential purchaser and his or her representatives will be interested in the last two to three years of your business plan. As they review it, they will try to answer the following questions: Did your business meet or exceed its plan? Did it fall below the plan? If so, was the senior management team aware of that and is there a good reason for missing it? The better you and your management team can show potential investors that you met your plan on a historical basis, the more solid you will seem; the more your team conveys the fact that it understands what's going on in the business, the more confident these buyers will feel in your business plans going forward.

Major products and potential obsolescence; low barrier to market entry. This is an interesting item in evaluating any transaction, because a lot of judgment is involved. In your industry, are the numbers continually going up? If so, odds are that you've got some pretty good products that your industry needs. What we in the advisory business often see, though, is that smaller companies can fly just under the radar screen of some of their larger and better capitalized competitors. Very often a larger company can simply take the small company out of the market by throwing money at new product development, effectively stealing the concept or idea that makes it unique. If you are selling something that the industry wants, the key players will attempt to get a similar product out to market faster than you can.

Wal-Mart is a good example. A schoolteacher invented Airborne, a cold remedy that fights germs and viruses. Very soon after it hit the market, Wal-Mart developed and began to sell its own version that threatened to cut into the sales of the original product and possibly put the teacher's company out of business. There was not a particularly high barrier to entry into the market for this product—it didn't need government approval or a long period of R&D—so development time wasn't a critical factor.

What if the larger company violates your intellectual property? My question to the owner of a closely held business is, do you have pockets deep enough to be able to defend an intellectual property suit? Probably not. I've seen such businesses die trying to defend a legitimate intellectual property claim.

Some larger companies won't even notice you're in their market space until you reach a level of sales that cuts into their market share. If you have $5 to $10 million in revenues in IBM's market space, IBM will not notice. But if you grow to $50 or $100 million in IBM's space and become a thorn in its side, it will notice and may attempt to rout you.

Sometimes a small company does the larger company a favor by conducting market research for it. If the smaller company proves there's a market for a certain product, the major manufacturer, which is better capitalized and has better distribution, might decide to develop its own version of that product, in which case the value of the smaller company will plummet. Why wouldn't the larger company just buy out the smaller company? Because it has done its SWOT analyses and by developing a product that is relatively easy to market, it's faster, cheaper, and easier for the larger company to invade the smaller company's market space than it is to take on all the issues that arise from a merger, such as integration, paperwork, and management and employee overlap. This is the build versus buy analysis mentioned above.

You need to understand what factors are out there that could take your specialty product out of the market. Investors in your company will be making the same evaluations.

Degree of real and potential competition. This is another good place to spot value in a company. Good companies have good competition. How do you evaluate how serious that competition is? As mentioned in Chapter 2, some business owners are naive in this area ("There's no business like my business"), but others are very savvy about who their competitors are. You want to be in that latter category when offering your company for sale. You not only want to be able to tell any potential investor who your biggest competitors are, but also who those competitors' major clients are and what those competitors are thinking about doing next. Smart business owners know that you keep your friends close and your enemies closer. You are probably engaged in some ongoing battles somewhere—maybe over customers or the poaching of employees—and you need to let potential investors know that you always have competitors on your radar screen. Knowing your competitors this well shows a degree of confidence about your business and its potential.

Major customers. This is a factor to which potential investors always pay extra special attention. Obviously you want to have a well-diversified customer base. The more blue chip clients a business owner has, with long-term histories with your company and good margins, the better. And you are going to get a premium for having those clients there. You always need to know to whom you are selling as well as to whom your competitors are selling. A business that has a lot of crossover clients with yours is not going be a business for which anyone will pay a premium. In fact, crossover clients can devalue a company because a competitor can actually poach from your customer base. You need to make sure that you know to whom you are selling and that you don't have that crossover.

Synergies. One item that potential purchasers will look for is whether, by doing the deal, they can cut costs without reducing sales volume. Can you truly enhance sales post-acquisition? Maybe. When speaking about synergies, everyone automatically thinks "oh, this is a great combo, 1 + 1 = 3." But if you don't do a good job of crunching the numbers, you could wind up with a deal that is not going to be additive and you will have a problem on your hands.

It goes back to valuation. You need to be mindful of that and do the math. Sometimes these can be very good deals, but other times people don't think it all the way through. In Chapter 8, we'll refer to the "village" it takes to close a deal, and one of your key players will be the accountants you hire to help you with the financial analyses.

Technologies. When you try to merge two companies that operate on different and incompatible technologies, you may be viewing a deal that can't pan out. The differing technologies can get in the way of getting the deal done. I've seen many mergers take longer than anticipated to become additive simply because the two entities had mismatched back office systems that couldn't communicate with each other. Time-consuming conflicts arose over which system would ultimately prevail.

Distribution and marketing. On the distribution side, your company might have lots of places to distribute its products—retail stores, the Internet, catalogs—and potential buyers might have another company that has a lot of products but not great distribution. Buyers would be interested in your company because they could take their products and drop them through your pipelines. The converse also can be true.

On the marketing side, often you see a smaller, closely held business that has the image of being the gold standard. Before potential players do an analysis of this company, they may assume they're dealing with a huge company only to learn that it is a $20 million company; smaller than they anticipated. These players might decide to acquire the company anyway to keep that brand and the marketing prowess of the name. Very often, they'll pay *up* for that brand and its marketing because they want to be able to acquire that gold standard.

The merger between Wachovia and First Union Bank is a good example. Wachovia had the better quality name recognition in the marketplace so the newly formed company kept that name, even though its current management is mostly from the First Union side. Such mergers also happen in the clothing industry. Liz Claiborne has built a fantastic platform of brands by acquiring or licensing well known lines—Juicy Couture, Dana Buchman, and Theory, for example—but most people don't realize that Liz Claiborne is the parent company because it has maintained the individual identities of the other brands to hold on to brand-loyal customer bases.

Have you established a business that has become the gold standard in your industry or niche market, but hesitate to let potential acquirers or investors in on the secret that your numbers are low? Hesitate no more: Investors might actually pay up for a small company with a great product reputation.

Employee compensation and benefits. This can be another great benefit of a strategic acquisition: If you've got a good company, chances are you have good employee benefits and employee costs. Benefits are a great place for investors to look for value in any company. One of the reasons is that if your company is applying best practices—that is, it is compensating employees and managers on the market and has vestment packages in place—buyers know that you understand employee retention issues and the chances are that those types of best practices are going to be carried on in other areas of the business. These best practices tell investors something about the values by which you conduct all areas of your business.

On the other hand, if they look at the numbers in the employee benefits area, and find your son-in-law drawing $100,000 a year and other employees drawing a salary who do no work there, then they will assume that there are other discrepancies in your company.

Antitrust implications. There are myriad rules and regulations that are outside the scope of this book. Potential buyers will hire good lawyers to help them in this area of strategic acquisitions. They want to ensure they are not violating any antitrust practices by creating a monopoly with a merger or acquisition. For example, let's say you have the largest packaging company on the East Coast and the buyer has the largest packaging company on the West Coast, and by combining the two companies it is going to have a lock on the market. The buyer might unintentionally create a monopoly—and that would probably be against the law.

Reputation of the seller and its management. In   my business, the investment banking business, the reputation of the seller is very important to the valuation of the company. Very often we see a company that has a "B" product but an "A+" management team and we can command a premium for that company, over a company that has an "A" product but a "C" reputation and is being run by "C" management. Investors will look for companies that are run by whatever the gold standard is in that industry.

Government regulations, environmental issues, and legal problems. These factors have been around for a while. Most companies have a few warts and some other problems, but that's okay. What's not okay is if they have a few problems of which the senior management team is not aware. The smart investors know that if these issues rear their ugly heads when they get well into the deal, or if they get so far as to have letters of intent on the table and then uncover these kinds of problems with your business, you are going to lose your credibility very quickly. Moreover, if you are aware of issues and haven't disclosed them and you've warranted certain things, you are going to have a lawsuit on your hands. The trick is to talk about these problems early in your discussions. Sometimes the deal might have to be postponed until a particular issue is cleared up, but if you know about it, you can work around it and it won't blow your deal out of the water.

Many deals blow up because of environmental issues, for instance. You always have to check for those. Often there are ways you can deal with them, though sometimes you can't. Sometimes the problem is part of an ongoing issue that investors will not want to touch. For example, if they get a report stating that a building they are buying has asbestos or lead paint, it may be too costly to remove it. That's a deal they might want to stay away from, unless they are willing to clean it up and then stick around long enough to recoup their costs, or have the sellers clean it up or agree to cover those costs. That's what risk management is all about. Companies like Marsh and McLennan evaluate these situations and figure out how to mitigate that risk and ensure against it. They calculate that they are going to be right a certain percentage of the time and that the times they miscalculate aren't going to disrupt their operations. These environmental issues can be very risky for a buyer of a company.

THE NEXT STEP

So you have completed your SWOT analyses and looked at all the factors that go into a merger or acquisition, and you have concluded that acquiring Company B is the smart strategic way to grow your business. There's only one missing piece: money. All your capital is tied up in your business and you have no resources with which to purchase the company. Should you give up on this pursuit? Not at all! In Chapters 4 and 5, we'll look at how to grow by using other people's money. To keep your business humming in the interim, to expand internally, or to buy new equipment—especially if you have uneven cash flow throughout the year—you may need to borrow money to keep things moving. To get to the next level, you need to understand that taking on some debt may smooth the transition from a closely held company to a powerhouse.

Debt Is *Not* a Dirty Word!

The reason most businesses fail or stagnate is that they are undercapitalized. It's common for busy business owners not to know how to leverage their own balance sheets, or worse, to be fearful of taking on debt. Many entrepreneurs think the fact that they don't have any debt is a good thing, but that's not necessarily true.

Think of your company as an asset. You want to make this asset work as hard as it possibly can. One of the ways to do that is through leverage. Another term for leverage is debt. To understand debt, just think of a home purchase. When you finance the purchase of a house with a home loan, you are leveraging what assets you have in order to do it and paying off the debt over time. You are leveraged when you are buying a house because it's not all your own money with which you're buying the house. When you put your $100,000 down on a house that costs $300,000, you leverage your assets with funds from a lender in order to make a bigger purchase than you could have afforded on your own. If you can't service the debt on the additional $200,000, the bank is going to come in and take it all—you'll lose your $100,000 and the house. But, if you pay the house off over time, and the property appreciates, then the gain realized when you sell is all yours.

From the moment you start your business, take out that second mortgage, or use your credit card, to the time that you launch an IPO and become a megacompany, you should constantly be looking for better, cheaper sources of capital. To do that properly, it's important that you understand all the different types of debt that are available to you and how to use each layer of debt effectively. This chapter gives you the information you need to understand why debt, although a four-letter word, is not a dirty word at all.

THE DIFFERENCE BETWEEN DEBT AND GROWTH CAPITAL

There is a big difference—and it's vital that you understand the difference—between *debt* (borrowing money that will be paid back with interest) and *growth capital* (offering equity in your company in exchange for an infusion of money). When you borrow money and go into debt, you are giving the lender your word—a bond (often accompanied by some collateral)—that you will eventually pay the money back. This lender will want to see its investment returned and know that it will get the return of the principal plus interest for the time you've held on to, and presumably made good use of, its money. That's the reason lenders put covenants into their agreement with you and why they ask for collateral (in case you default). On the other hand, growth capital, which we'll focus on in Chapter 5, is money that is invested in exchange for part ownership of your company that is expected to be paid back through the growth of your company, the same way we expect growth in our stock market investments.

Debt capital can take many different forms. Each form has a very different purpose, but understanding how to use debt properly can be very important as you plan your company's growth.

THE TOP FIVE THINGS LENDERS LOOK FOR IN A COMPANY

1. Established business
2. Positive cash flow
3. Three years of financial statements (preferably audited)
4. Assets they can securitize
5. Solid business plan

As an entrepreneur and business owner you must be comfortable with managing cash flow. If you are not comfortable managing money, you are going to have a hard time managing your company's cash flow and investing and reinvesting properly, so you really need to get comfortable with your company's cash flow and how businesspeople look at debt.

Many of the same rules that apply to your personal finances apply to getting debt capital for a business. In the world of personal finance, if you have no experience with credit, it's going to be very difficult to get those first loans. But if you can demonstrate that you've exercised good judgment and you understand how to manage the money and the debt you are taking on, then you won't have a problem getting loans when you are ready to take on more debt because you've already demonstrated your knowledge and your ability.

It's *exactly* the same in business.

WHY GO INTO DEBT?

One of the stereotypes many lenders have about entrepreneurs is that they are averse to debt. While that may be a good thing in your personal life, knowing how to leverage your company's balance sheet, where and when to go to the bank, and what nontraditional opportunities are available to finance the growth of your business are crucial to the health of your company. Lenders and investors do not necessarily look at debt as bad for the business, particularly when it can help lead to increased growth for your business and potential profits for you.

This chapter focuses only on debt because one of the problems that owners of closely held businesses have that keeps them from growing is that they don't understand how to use debt effectively. You have to make sure you can service your debt. If you can't service it, or if you have growth plans that won't provide enough cash flow to service the debt, you'll need to examine your business model in order to decide if there's a hole in the model or if you need to capitalize with equity instead. Because entrepreneurs typically don't understand how to use debt, they don't take on debt and they don't leverage the assets of their company, which hinders the growth of their businesses.

STAGES OF GROWTH/ STAGES OF NEED

As your business grows, you will experience various stages of financial need.

Starting up your business. At this stage, your business may be no more than a "twinkle in your eye," a great idea that's just waiting to take shape. During this stage, you will need money called seed capital to fuel your idea and start up your business. Seed capital can come from various sources, including:

- Personal resources
- Friends and family
- Angel investors
- Small business loans
- Investment companies
- Credit cards
- Home equity loans

Second-stage growth. Once your business gets going, you will need second-stage financing to expand your company and ensure it remains an ongoing concern. This kind of financing also can come through many sources, including:

- Angel investors
- State-sponsored venture capital/grants
- Private venture capital
- Strategic alliances
- Small Business Investment Companies (SBICs)
- SBA loans

Mature financing. This stage separates the empire builder from the lifestyle maker, because as your business matures, you need to either become well capitalized and grow to the next level or develop an exit strategy. You've overtaken the competition and saturated your market and now the only way for your business to increase profitability is to grow through new product development, expansion into new markets, acquisition of another company, or to be bought by a bigger, better-capitalized company. The money to finance this kind of expansion or exit can come from taking your business public (in the form of an IPO), private equity, venture capital companies, or an outright sale.

This chapter deals with *first-stage expansion* of your business (or any kind of expansion post-start-up but before explosive growth) and guides you through the various types of debt capital available. Remember, we are assuming that some debt is a plus for the company. Providing your repay your loan on time:

- You have cash with which to grow while still maintaining control over your business.
- You avoid dilution of ownership.
- You can deduct the costs of that debt from your business revenues and keep all the resulting profits.

First-stage expansion takes some explaining—it does not necessarily come a year or two after starting your business. It could come at *any* point in the life of your company when you realize you've got a good business model and have good cash flow but it's not enough to keep the engines running at full speed. You have enough revenues to service the cost of the debt and want to expand without taking on partners or investors.

■ REMEMBER

The number of years your company is in business has nothing to do with the stage the business is at in terms of its growth. I recently worked with a client who has a business that is about nine years old. You would not normally think of a nine-year-old company as an early-stage business, but because of the size of the business's revenues and its geographic footprint, the private equity and venture investors still consider it an early-stage business—it's not really mature, it's not really large, and it hasn't scaled yet.

So, after start-up, why would you need more money for your business? Some reasons include:

- *Adding new products or services to your business mix*
- *Business expansion and acquisition.* You've got a great opportunity to expand your markets and, hence, your profits.
- *Capital improvements.* In order to stay competitive, you need to upgrade anything from your computer systems to your warehouses to your methods of distribution that only an infusion of capital can buy.
- *Debt repayment.* You need to borrow money to repay a previous debt.
- *Equity repurchase.* You want to or must regain control of your business by buying out partners.
- *Working capital.* You need cash to keep your business running in the wake of an unexpected and temporary shortfall of revenues.

THREE KEY POINTS
ABOUT DEBT

First key point. Clearly the time to get money is when you don't need money. When your business is going well and everything is humming along, you want to be making a focused effort to talk to banks about how great your company is, how well you are growing, and how strong your earnings are. You want to be out there telling *that* story and getting the bankers very comfortable with *you.* If you begin this process when you are in a crisis, no one will want to come and rescue you because from the lender's viewpoint, a rescue is a risky proposition.

Second key point. Once you have a relationship with a lender, it's very important to do two things:

1. *Stay very close to that lender and keep it apprised of your company's financial situation.* Make sure you meet with the lender on a quarterly basis; make sure the lender or the institution is up to speed on what's going on with your business and that they understand it. If you think you are going to run into a bump along the way, prepare the lender for that news very, very early. Start working with the lender; don't try to hide the bad news, don't mask it. See if you can work with them to become a part of the solution.

2. *Even if you have a good lending relationship with a bank, you need to develop other such relationships.* You need to start talking with other institutions because each lender looks at a credit profile differently. Even within the same organization, there may be different groups that look at credit differently. Not every lender is right for you at every stage of the growth of your business. It goes back to the first key point: you can't ask for the money when you need it. You have to build those relationships when things are going very well so that a variety of lenders have trust and confidence in you *before* you ask them to lend you money and before they will

actually do it. Like all relationships, those relationships take time to establish, build, and nurture.

Most business owners don't realize this. They are very busy and they think that if they already have a bank behind their business they won't need to worry about money when the need arises. But you need to always be talking to a variety of lenders.

Third key point. When you borrow money, your lender becomes, in a very real sense, your business partner and part of your financial management team. As you move into having professional relationships and using debt and equity (other people's money, which we discuss in Chapter 5), you want your lenders to understand your business as well as you do. You want to make your lenders your partners even if you retain complete control. While you need to have your management team, your employees, and your clients—the people who make the business's wheels turn every day—you also have to have those people who will help your business jump to the next level. Some of those partners are internal and some are external. Chapter 8 discusses the different people it takes to make your business grow.

The bottom line. It is vital to understand the connection between debt and your business relationships. Get comfortable with your balance sheet and understand the way banks look at it. (More about that later in this chapter.) It's important to understand what's going on in the mind of the guy sitting on the other side of the desk. That's where business owners and entrepreneurs sometimes stumble; they are so excited about their business that they don't understand what the lender has to do to evaluate that business. As a result, the business owner may get turned down because the banker does not want to have to go to the loan committee to discuss something that is not working out well. These lenders are accountable for every penny they lend. If you understand how lenders are being judged (and they are being graded!), you'll do yourself (and them) a big favor by giving them the information they need, presented exactly the way they need it. Then, and only then, can they help you if you do hit some bumps down the road.

DIFFERENT KINDS OF DEBT

Now that you understand your business's need for debt, you need to get comfortable with the various kinds of debt.

Debt comes in many forms, with lots of different labels such as senior debt, junior debt, subordinated debt, high-yield debt, and unsecured debt. The difference is the pecking order of who gets paid back first. If something happens to your company and you have to liquidate, what the lender cares about is liquidation preference: who gets paid back and in what order.

Senior debt most often includes funds borrowed from banks, insurance companies, merchant banks, or other financial institutions, as well as notes, bonds, or debentures that are not expressly defined as junior or subordinated debt. This chapter focuses on senior debt; Chapter 5 will explain the other kinds of debt and how they can be useful in your growth plans.

This section discusses the different kinds of debt you might want to consider as you grow your business. When you approach various lenders, you have to know what kind of loan you are seeking.

Fixed-asset acquisition. Buying fixed assets of another company can help you grow your business and provide assets that you need but don't have. In this kind of acquisition, you buy the assets of a company or selected assets of the company, versus the whole company, which would be a stock purchase. Let's say you want to acquire a new piece of machinery for your plant. That's a fixed asset. It will depreciate on your balance sheet, so why not lease it? You have to weigh whether it's better to buy or lease. In addition, not everything is leasable.

Lease financing. The way to figure out whether to buy or lease is to determine what the residual value is at the end of the equipment's life. For instance, I don't know why anyone would buy a computer versus leasing a computer. By the end of the lease term the technology has changed and the used computer has no value; therefore, leasing is the better option. Sometimes it's more convenient and cost-effective to lease your equipment rather than buy it. When you lease, you do *not* have to lay out tons of cash and you can always trade the equipment in for the latest models and updates.

Bond financing. Let's say you want to buy some land to build a new warehouse or plant. You may be able to issue a small industrial development bond and raise money that way. Often state and local governments offer this kind of financing because you are going to create jobs that will extend their tax base.

Insurance company financing. Insurance companies also lend money, so you often can borrow money from insurance companies through private placements. A private placement is a negotiated deal with an insurance company either for debt or equity in your business. Typically with an insurance company, it's for debt. Why? Insurance companies prefer a debt structure that matches their assets (investments) against their liabilities (expected claims), and that's much harder to do with an equity investment.

Factoring. Quite often when a company is experiencing a cash flow crunch and has been refused a loan from a bank, it will turn to a factoring company. The factor is going to assume the credit risk from the company's customers for a price—a very high price. When you put a factor on something, the lender gives you the money for an "open to buy." For example, suppose you have to buy inventory once a quarter and you need $250,000 every quarter to buy your inventory, yet you don't have that kind of cash flow. The lender will give you the money up front and then will factor the repayment so it's kind of like revolving credit. Normally you would be able to borrow and use your inventory to secure your credit line; however, in some cases—for example, in the garment or retail industries where the inventories may not be worth much in liquidation—there is often not much choice but to factor. If a clothing retailer goes bust, how much is that $250,000 inventory really worth at the end of the season? Ten cents on the dollar? That is why when the factor puts up the money so that you can buy all the inventory you need or want, it charges you a factor on that inventory that continues to rotate. For instance, a factor can charge you 10 percent above what you paid for the inventory. That means to benefit from a factoring arrangement, a clothing retailer would have to sell every item every season, which rarely happens. The problem with factoring is that it is very difficult to pay off this kind of loan. But, despite this difficulty, it's a very common form of debt, especially in the clothing business. You almost have to sell your company in order to pay off the debt, so factors can wind up basically owning your company if you are not careful.

I have a friend who is a very talented shoe designer and a smart businesswoman, but she must rely on factors at times because fashions change quickly and she must put out the next new line even if it means getting stuck with old inventory she can't sell. The point is that you want to avoid factoring if you can. Sometimes, however, factoring is the only way to go. Lots of manufacturers will be the factors for you because it's very lucrative for them and it keeps *you* in the game.

Is factoring for you? The advantages are that it reduces the working capital you need to grow a business; you are limited only by the business's sales and receivables, not cash flow or financial position; and a factoring relationship normally transfers all or most of the credit risk associated with receivables to the factor, and thus may reduce your cost of credit and collection functions.

The disadvantage of factoring is that it's expensive relative to other forms of debt because the factor assumes the credit risk and administration of receivables. Not all account receivables may be acceptable to the factor.

Mezzanine financing. This is what I like to call patient capital and it's really a hybrid between debt and equity. Mezzanine financing has an equity orientation and a debt orientation. There are two different types of mezzanine financing: debt and equity. We'll get into this more in Chapter 5.

Typically, mezzanine players are going to be looking at an 18 to 25 percent annual internal rate of return, which is quite high. And the way they are going to get that is by lending you the money with a much higher coupon; usually they are going to get somewhere between a 12 and 14 percent coupon and then they are going to take a warrant in the company— an equity kicker—that makes up the difference between the 12 to 14 percent and the 18 to 25 percent. It goes back to the fact that banks don't lend growth capital. Banks make loans for working capital, often against assets or with a personal guarantee. For instance, banks will help finance inventory and they will finance tangible assets, but they are not going to lend you growth capital. Mezzanine lenders are interested in companies that grow and they expect to make a nice return off that equity kicker. So if you have good cash flow and are in a growth mode, mezzanine lenders are a nice way to get the money you need and, if everything works out, your lenders will be happy to get the nice return and you will still control every aspect of your business.

Layered financing. If you think about public companies, you realize they are built on layered financing, and you can build your company that way too. That means you will have to assume senior debt *and* subordinated debt. As your business grows, you may also decide to float bonds and issue preferred stocks that are layered in; that is, you have multiple layers of financing with different interest rates and different covenants governing the repayment of the money.

VIEW YOURSELF AS
YOUR LENDER VIEWS YOU

Asking yourself the same questions a bank or another lender would ask allows you to focus on the issues you need to think about before seeking loans. Here are some issues that banks consider when thinking about lending money to business owners:

- What is the purpose of the required financing?
- How much financing will be needed and for how long?
- What type of collateral is the business able to provide?
- At what stage of growth is the business?
- In what industry is the business?
- Does the business qualify for government financing?
- What are the company's goals (SWOT)?
- Is the owner willing to personally guarantee the debt?
- How much is the owner willing to spend to obtain the financing?

- How much debt can the company support based on its cash flow?
- What types of covenants can the company handle without restricting it effectiveness?

Bankers look at all of these factors as they try to assess how they impact your company.

How Banks Think

When banks lend their money, they are looking for return *of* their principal and a return *on* their principal. They're not lending growth capital—that's what equity investors do. Think of a bank as a bond and think of private equity, or mezzanine investors, as a stock. Once you start looking at banks that way, you realize that the amount that they are willing to lend you and the rate at which they are willing to lend it to you correlates directly to how much risk they think they're taking. Hence, the old adage, the banks will only lend you money when you don't need it.

■ REMEMBER

That the bank is always weighing the worst-case scenario. In the event that the unthinkable happens, where do lenders want to be in the repayment schedule? Senior lenders always want to be put first in the pecking order. If a bank wants to be first and thinks there's a chance something bad might happen, it is going to demand a higher interest rate and require more collateral and more onerous covenants in the loan agreement. If the bank thinks a loan to you is a sure thing with no repayment problems, then it will be much looser in its terms.

Banks are always critically evaluating how a variety of circumstances would impact them. That's how they look at any loan request you make.

How to Prepare Financials for the Bank

Banks are looking for lots of different things in your financials. Here are some of the details you need to present to them:

- At least your last three years of financials, with every "i" dotted and every "t" crossed. If you've had any ups and downs or gaps in your earnings history, then you want to have them noted, with a rationale for these anomalies. In fact, you want to have an explanation for any exception to a stellar earnings pattern. Audited statements are recommended. To the degree that you can have your financials audited, it's a good idea to show proof of audits to the bank.
- A very clear listing of all of your business's hard assets, because they can be used as collateral.
- Proper documentation, so that if they ask you for something, you aren't scrambling. These documents could include titles, deeds to property owned by your busi-

ness, and contracts—anything that impacts your company's financial status.

How to Negotiate the Best Terms

The way to negotiate the best terms on anything is to have options. If there is no competition, it's going to be very difficult to have any kind of negotiation. What I recommend to people is, even if you are very happy with your banking relationship, get out there and start talking to other bankers. Start developing other relationships so that you will have options when it is time to negotiate loan terms.

There are a couple of reasons for doing this. First, you won't know what else is available until you talk to a number of people. Second, if you do need to move to another bank in the future, you won't be starting from scratch to build that relationship.

The best banks are the ones with which you have the most solid relationships because, at the end of the day, they are banking on you! It's very difficult to establish a good relationship when you are trying to make a transition in your business. Relationships have to be developed over time.

How to Determine the Right Bank for You

Not every bank is good for you at every stage of your business. When you're starting out, for instance, you might be comfortable with a smaller bank with which you have a strong, personal relationship. If it is the local bank in your town and you have a solid reputation and a good repayment history, the bank may be willing to lend you some start-up money. That bank may not be willing to take a whole lot of risk, but it might be willing to be flexible because it knows you and your track record.

But as you grow your business, your needs are going to change. You are not going to be willing to be the security on that loan anymore, and you may need to finance different types of things. Some banks, for instance, may be stronger in lease financing; some may only do back-to-back lending; some banks may be sophisticated enough and able to analyze risk well enough to combine asset-based lending with cash flow and create a senior structure that is a little bit different from a totally secured senior structure, allowing the loan to be senior on your books as opposed to subordinated. Why would that be important? Because banks don't lend subordinated money! And, as you grow, subordinated debt may be what you need. If you can get it through a bank, you may be able to avoid a mezzanine financer, who will lend you money at much higher rates than a bank and will also expect you to repay the original loan.

Some banks have limits on how much they can lend to any one customer. So if you are in a real expansion mode and you know that will continue for the foreseeable future, you want to make sure you are with a lender that can meet your demand. You don't want to be constantly bumping up against its limits.

And of course, the larger the bank, the more likely it is to have these options available *internally*. A good accounting firm and a good attorney that works with businesses that are growing are going to have relationships with larger banks.

One of the things you should do is talk to them when you start *thinking* about growing, not when you are ready to go. In doing so you can get the process started, gather information, develop the relationships, and become knowledgeable about how borrowing money will impact your business.

And of course, the larger the bank, the more likely it is to have these options available internally. A good accounting firm and a good attorney that works with businesses that are growing are going to have relationships with larger banks. One of the things you should do is talk to them when you start thinking about growing, not when you are ready to go. In doing so you can get the process started, gather information, develop the relationships, and become knowledgeable about how borrowing money will impact your business.

■ REMEMBER

Once you start to finance your company, you are always going to be refinancing your company, because you are always going to be looking for better and cheaper sources of capital. That is why it is important to find a bank—or several banks—whose lending capabilities match the size and the stage of your business.

OTHER FORMS OF FINANCING

Banks aren't the only source of money for your business. There are a lot of different kinds of lenders out there. There are people who do very interesting types of structures; for example, the securitization of revenue streams from licenses and royalty agreements, or convertible notes, or structures that exchange a higher coupon (interest rate) for lending on an unsecured basis. Again, this goes back to my point about getting out there and having the conversation.

Rock star David Bowie is one of the more famous examples of someone selling off their future revenue streams. He agreed to sell the future royalties from his records, concerts, and film archives in exchange for ready cash that he and his financial advisors could invest as they saw fit. Wall Street coined the term Bowie Bonds to describe this type of deal. The U.S. government does a similar thing when it sells Ginnie Mae home loans, as do the quasi-governmental agencies Freddie Mac and Fannie Mae.

And don't forget about finance companies such as GE Capital or American Express. They are in the business of lending money to business owners, and might be a source of funds for your company.

In addition to bank (debt) financing and lease financing, there are other ways to raise money to finance your business.

Government-Sponsored Financing

There are a number of options available to entrepreneurs through government agencies, depending on the nature of your business. The well-known government loan programs available to business owners include:

- SBA LowDoc program
- SBA Express program

- SBA CAP Lines program
- International trade loan program
- Export working capital program
- Certified development company (504 or CRD loan)
- Department of Housing and Urban Development (HUD)
- Department of Agriculture
- State and city industrial development or economic development programs

The advantages of these programs are that they are a ready source of funds, the loans usually come with lower interest rates than you could find at a bank, and there are lower collateral requirements. The disadvantages are that the loans are very complex and may involve a lot of time-consuming research and paperwork on your part. There is usually a lengthy approval and closing process, thus making the loan cumbersome to plan for and excluding you from making quick use of the money. There may also be intense competition for funding. Know that these government-sponsored loans are a lot of work, but ultimately may be very worthwhile.

Asset Financing

Common types of asset-based financing are accounts receivable, inventory, and fixed-asset financing. Each is based on the worth of your company and may involve a lien on your future revenues if you fail to repay on time.

Five C's of Credit

There are five key elements a borrower should have to obtain credit:

- Character (integrity)
- Capacity (sufficient cash flow to service the obligation)
- Capital (net worth)
- Collateral (assets to secure the debt)
- Conditions (of the borrower and the overall economy)

THE DOWNSIDE OF DEBT

Debt is a wonderful way for you to expand your business and keep control of it at the same time. The downside is that the business owes the debt and must repay on time to avoid expensive penalties. Such repayments reduce your cash flow and profit.

Again, here's the important point about debt: You always want to look for the best and the cheapest sources of money. There's something called leveraged recapitalization, which we'll explore in Chapter 5. In a "leveraged recap," the private equity guys come in, invest in the firm, let the buyer take some chips off the table, and then go out and refinance the transaction with the cheapest money they can structure, usually debt capital, hence the term *leveraged recap*. What they do is take their own equity *out* and replace it with the bank's or the lender's loan, at a much lower rate of interest—and they didn't have to give up any equity for it.

Constantly finding better and cheaper sources of debt capital is the way the big companies think and, if you want to grow your business into a bigger business, it should be the way you think too. That's the reason you need to build and nurture these lender relationships and be out there and always talking to professionals.

DEBT VERSUS EQUITY CAPITAL

When things are going well, though, and you are growing at comfortable or explosive rates, another equally effective way to infuse your company with working capital is to use other people's money (OPM). OPM is usually equity capital; it's turning your lenders into investors in your company. That's what equity capital is: taking on someone with an ownership stake. In other words, when the bank lends you money to buy your house, it doesn't own your house with you. It has made a loan to you. It will take your house away from you if you default on that loan, but you own your house as long as you pay the mortgage. When you take on equity capital, your lenders own a piece of the rock. Why would you want to give away a piece of the rock? Because you need capital to grow and you don't have the cash flow to sustain your debt.

Is this a bad thing? Not necessarily. We'll explore this issue in Chapter 5.

FACTORS TO CONSIDER WHEN REVIEWING TYPES OF DEBT FINANCING

The table in Figure 4.1 outlines the characteristics of various types of financing. As you are trying to determine which type will work best for your business, consider the following questions:

- What is the purpose of the required debt financing?
- How much debt financing is needed and for how long?
- What type of collateral is the business able to provide?
- At what growth stage is the business in its life cycle?
- In what industry does the business operate?
- Does the business qualify for government financing?
- What are the company's goals for the future?
- How much is the business willing to pay to obtain debt financing?
- Are the business owners willing to guarantee debt?
- What amount of debt financing will the business cash flow support?
- With what types of debt covenants can the business effectively function?

FIGURE 4.1 *Summary of Characteristics of Common Types of Financing*

Source	Purpose	Security	Evaluation Criteria	Advantages	Disadvantages
Banks	Working capital, term loans	Accounts receivable, inventory, equipment, etc.	5 C's of credit	Lower interest rates; no ownership dilution	Difficult to qualify; restrictive covenants
Leasing	Facilities and equipment	Facilities and equipment	Value of collateral	Various financial, accounting, and income tax benefits	Higher implicit interest rates; no benefit from asset residual values
Government-sponsored	Varies by program	Varies by program	Varies by program	Favorable rates and terms; financing opportunities for businesses that might not qualify for other financing	Complex paperwork; lengthy time delays; contractual and legal requirements
Asset-based loans	Working capital, term loans	Accounts receivable, inventory, equipment	Value of collateral	Easier to obtain than traditional bank loans	Expensive
Factoring	Working capital	Accounts receivable	Value of receivables	Easier to obtain than traditional bank loans; reduces collection efforts	Expensive

CHAPTER FIVE

Other People's Money

There comes a time in the life of every company where meaningful growth can't happen without truly capitalizing the company. You begin to realize that organic growth is not enough, so you begin to look at M&A opportunities. Or you may have some major capital expenditures such as replacing equipment. Whatever the reason, you need money—the kind of money that cares about a business's growth potential, not simply about getting principal back with a small return. In other words, you've realized it takes money to make money.

If you look at the big boys—the public companies—you realize that along with creating liquidity for the founders, they do an IPO to get at the capital tied up in the company so they can continue their growth.

Dig deeper and you are likely to find that many public companies have layers and layers of capital they have sourced from everywhere—banks, private investors, public debt offerings, secondary stock issues, etc.

Why would you need more capital than you can possibly generate at your current level of business?

- You may want to acquire another company, a competitor, a supplier, or a vendor.
- You may want to enter a new market or to develop a new product.
- You may need to attract bigger and more powerful talent in order to stay competitive in your industry.

Any of these objectives may require more capital than your company currently generates.

When you look at your business from a strategic point of view, some good questions to ask are: Can I solve this problem by throwing money at it? Would more money achieve this particular goal or allow me to seize an attractive opportunity? Is there another way to address these issues? Many times you can work out clever ways to overcome the need to bring in more capital—strategic partnerships and alliances, license agreements, securitizing various revenue streams— but very often you simply need more money.

Why wouldn't you go out and borrow the money? Because you don't have enough cash flow. You can take on debt only if you can pay it off with your cash flow, or if you have the assets to protect it. At this stage in the game, what you really need is growth capital—money that understands the risks and rewards of high-growth businesses.

As we learned in Chapter 4, debt is about paying back the capital borrowed at a fixed rate. Think of it as you would a bond in your portfolio. You own the bond not so much for the price appreciation but for the certainty that you will get your principal back and earn a little extra along the way. The money we are speaking of here is equity capital. People and companies who invest this type of capital expect their investment dollars to appreciate, the same way you would when you put a new stock into your personal portfolio.

THE UPSIDE OF OPM

Besides rapid growth, there is a real advantage to taking on growth capital that many business owners don't understand: When you take on equity capital, you often get much more than just money. If you take on the right kind of equity capital, you get access to advice, resources, and often human capital that you did not have before.

For example, suppose you have a company that runs a small regional restaurant or retail chain and you've decided that your chain should franchise around the country. You've done your homework and realize your concept will play well in Atlanta, Chicago, and Dallas. If you find a financial sponsor (private equity and/or mezzanine investor) who has successfully rolled out stores in these markets, you will have gained more than just a financial partner. You will now be in business with someone who has "been there, done that." Your new investor will already have the right real estate model in place, as well as the contacts and resources in your new markets to help you execute your strategy expediently. Your new equity partner might have internal talent to lend you as well. Wouldn't it be great to get not only the growth capital but also operational expertise as well?

There may be many other benefits as well: your financial partners can cut the time it would take for you to execute well in these new markets by knowing what the local flavor is, the local business climate, the legal obstacles, who to contact to speed up the process, and so on. Remember, these investors are not simply being magnanimous; these resources are part of their business strategy—seeking to invest in companies where they can add value. Just go to any of their Web sites and you'll see what I mean.

These investors also can offer resources in the areas of sourcing and manufacturing and becoming a global player. Currently, we see many private equity firms opening offices in China, Hong Kong, and India, markets that are key to the long-term survival of any business. Are these investors looking for opportunities for themselves? Yes, of course, but by understanding how to make it happen in a foreign environment, they can cut your learning curve and the learning curve of their other portfolio companies as well.

So, if you are smart about how you do it, you get much more than just money.

THE DOWNSIDE OF OPM

Not all business owners are candidates for growth capital. If you are going to take on other people's money, you need to understand that you are going to have a very serious business partner, someone to whom you will be accountable and responsible. That accountability could be a reason that you don't want to do it. Some entrepreneurs are great at making the business happen and managing it in their own unique way, but they are not willing or able to report in on a quarterly basis or make regular management meetings. These business owners are *not* good candidates for private equity—even if they have the most A+ company in the world—because they don't want to take on a business partner.

Let's get down to the nitty gritty details of OPM.

RAISING GROWTH CAPITAL: WHAT IT TAKES

For a growing business, capital is the equivalent of oxygen. All too often, businesses start out undercapitalized and fail to take the necessary steps to ensure that an opportunity will not be missed just because they can't afford to take advantage of it.

Taking on other people's money is not for the faint of heart, because with it comes not only the expectation from investors that you will meet annual growth and earnings targets, but the understanding that your company is an asset in their portfolios, and must be treated in a businesslike manner.

When you put your money in a mutual fund that invests in publicly traded companies, you expect to get a certain return over a certain period of time and, of course, you want to be able to get your money out. The same goes for venture, mezzanine, and private equity lenders in your business. Think of these sources of growth capital like a mutual fund for institutions that want to invest in private companies. They have criteria as to stage, size, and often industry or geography that guide their investment decisions, and they have return hurdles they must meet for investors who, in most cases, are limited partners in their fund.

The Five M's

A venture capitalist friend of mine, Kathy Harris, is a partner with Noro Mosley Ventures in Atlanta. Kathy tells her prospective clients that to be successful at raising growth capital, their companies must have the five M's: management, market, money, mettle, and magic. Briefly, we'll look at why each of these factors matter in the capital raising process.

Management. In business, it's all about management, management, management. Look at your current team in light of how you are going to execute your plan once you get funded. If you had the money right now!—are these the people that you would choose to move the company forward? A lot of times the team—including you—that got your company to a certain level is not the team that can execute the accelerated growth goals an investor wants to achieve.

Management is the single most important factor in determining whether or not you are investment-worthy. Be realistic. If you need to, shore up the management team now, or at least identify key players who would be willing to come on board at the time of funding. I often think of the entrepreneur as the centrifugal force that holds the company together, steering the values, vision, and culture of the organization. All around this force are the members of the team that make it happen. Key players from the investors' point of view will be finance, operations, and—depending on the type of business—merchandising, sales, product development, etc. Without this team in place, or identified, it will be difficult to convince investors that you can execute a realistic and rapid growth plan.

Market. You need to understand what investors mean when they ask you about the market. For example, if you have developed proprietary accounting software for the financial services market, don't talk about the market for accounting software in general. Likewise, are you a market leader or at least well-positioned to overtake the leader? Investors are looking for companies that offer products and services that fill a void, or solve a problem better than what is currently available. If you don't have competition or are not solving a major problem, then there's probably not a big enough market for your product or service to offer investors a suitable return.

Money. Your company needs to be making money. In today's environment, it is all about growing the bottom line. Margins matter here too. Investors are interested in companies that they believe can grow their market share and increase their bottom line, or EBITDA growth, without eroding margins. If your strategy is simply volume—to sell more—that *will* not be attractive to potential investors. Here's why. Low-margin businesses offer no cushion in the event of a business downturn or miscalculation of the plan. Additionally, low margins are a sign that customers do not value the products or services and are not willing to pay a premium for them. Which would you bet on, the horse that always wins by a nose or the one who finishes lengths ahead of the competition every time he races?

Mettle. Mettle is the strength that it takes to work your plan each and every day. Owning a business is not easy. When you own a business, you are the one who stays up at night sweating the payroll, figuring out how you are going to finance the next big move, and worrying about the competition. And when you take on the task of raising capital and answering to a board and investors, you have just raised the bar tenfold. Just as some employees could never own a company because they don't want to worry if their check will be there on Friday, not all business owners have the fortitude to take on the fiduciary responsibility of other people's money.

Magic. The last piece of the puzzle is the magic. It is the "intangible extra" that lets the investor know that you and your team have what it takes to hit a home run. Some call it chemistry, but every growth company that receives backing from investors has something that investors think will be the secret to their success.

So why does a company take on growth capital in the first place? Why would any business owner want the additional headache and sleepless nights? Remember, business is about money, and it takes money to make money. Companies such as Tiffany & Co., Dunkin' Donuts, Reddy Ice, and PayPal all had private equity behind them. Virtually every company that you can name that has been able to grow exponentially has been able to do so because it was well capitalized. Ask yourself who are your biggest competitors and why? Chances are they are companies to which your customers feel more comfortable giving larger orders. Why? Because the larger order is not going to strip them of all of their resources, either in terms of financial or human capital. Their management team is sophisticated, and they can afford the systems and controls necessary to get the job done. Why? Because they have money!

DETERMINING SUCCESS AT RAISING CAPITAL

How does a company decide if it can be successful at raising growth capital? Speak with an investment banker. Investment bankers typically are paid only a small fee up front. They earn their money from successfully completing a deal or raising capital, so the good ones will tell you honestly what they think the chances of success are, and what you might be able to do before hiring a banker to help ensure your chance of success. As stated earlier, don't try to go it alone. All too often we hear from companies that a slew of investors have been after them to give them capital. The reality is, most of the time, these discussions have not gotten to a serious level, the prospective investors have not had an opportunity to look at the financials of the company, and the company has not been properly prepared to speak to investors. Raising capital is a time-intensive process. There is a reason that even the big companies, banks, and investment banking firms hire outside firms to represent them when they are working on a transaction!

SOURCES OF OPM

There are many sources of OPM (see Figure 5.1), but in this chapter we discuss three main kinds:

1. Venture capitalists
2. Private equity funds
3. Mezzanine lenders

Let's look at these main sources of capital in a bit more depth.

Venture Capitalists

Venture capital (VC) is a catchall term that describes an illiquid equity investment in a privately held company. The company may need seed, development, or early or later-stage capital; but in all cases, to secure an investment, you will need to convince potential VC investors of your company's ability to execute a high-growth strategy.

It used to be that you went to venture capitalists (VCs) with a business plan, they gave you $25 million, and off you went. That is not what VCs are really about today. VCs are looking for real businesses in which to invest. They are

FIGURE 5.1 *Capital Sources Appropriate for Size and*
Stage of Business

Stage	Capital Needed	Source
Start-up, prerevenue	$0–$500,000	Friends and family
Seed, under $1mm	$500,000–$5mm	Angel investors and funds
Early growth, EBITDA positive	$5mm–$20mm	Venture capital funds, mezzanine lenders
Expansion	$20mm+	Private equity, buyout funds

looking for ideas that they can readily understand and a
clear path to growth and expansion. They are willing, however, to look at earlier stage businesses or those that are already up and running that have a management team they
can believe in to execute its vision, and are positioned to
scale rapidly. Remember, in this context "early stage" is
not about years in business; it refers to the maturity of
what you have in place as far as a plan, talent, customers,
intellectual property, barriers to entry, and other factors
concerned.

VCs are willing to come in with earlier-stage capital that
can aggressively move a company along. They may stay with
that company all the way to the eventual exit or IPO. They
may exit to a private equity firm that infuses more capital on
the way to an eventual IPO or they may recapitalize it themselves. But, typically, VCs are looking for earlier-stage busi-

nesses that have the potential for extraordinarily high growth, such as high-tech, biotech, and similar high-growth ventures that need to be funded aggressively in order to execute efficiently.

Private Equity

The private equity world is interested in solid, well-established companies that already have a long, profitable operating history; a strong management team; a repeatable, sustainable revenue model; and a clear expansion strategy. These companies have a clear vision and strategy toward growth, but they lack the capital necessary to get the business where it needs to be: that is, over the hurdle to the next level of growth. Great examples of companies that exploded under the watchful eye of private equity investors are Tommy Bahama, P.F. Changs, Sherman Williams, and Morton's.

What private equity investors are good at is capitalizing the business in such a way that they can unleash the power of the business. Their exit may be an IPO, a sale to a strategic investor, or further recapitalization of the business. They are not interested in early stage businesses. Private equity groups (PEGs) are looking to back experienced management teams. They are looking for solid track records and, for the most part, good clean companies. They expect to earn their return on their investment in a company over a three-to-seven-year holding period. Usually, they are not looking to turn around a company that's in trouble (although there is a whole group of funds out there that focus on distressed and turnaround situations).

What the private equity firms look for in an M&A transaction:

- Ability to generate cash flow from their investment
- Ability to create a profitable exit strategy
- High minimum rates of return
- Specific investment horizons
- Well-structured management
- Consistent earnings
- Excellent reputation in the industry
- Solid market position

Often in family-owned businesses, the company has been in existence for many years and when the next generation comes in, it wants to grow the business to the next level. The business may be operationally sound but its balance sheet is constrained from years of operating too conservatively or fueling all its growth organically. This younger generation will turn to a private equity firm to recapitalize the business, often creating much-needed liquidity for the first generation and positioning the company for its next leg up.

At this point, it's useful to know where these funds—VCs and PEGs—get their money to invest. Before you go out to the markets and bring in this kind of capital, you have to understand why they have the kinds of growth expectations that they have for returns. Just as you are seeking out investors in your business, VCs and PEGs seek out investors who share their vision and have the money to invest.

People who put their money into VC and private equity funds are looking for very high returns, better returns than they can get in the public equity market. One of the reasons that they're paid so well is that there's no liquidity for them, from their investment in the portfolio companies, until there is a liquidity event—a sale, recapitalization, or IPO of the portfolio company. Another way to look at PEGs is as if they are giant mutual funds, with different parameters to invest in private companies. Just as mutual funds have differing investment criteria—high growth, income, or a particular focus, such as investments in a specific geographical area—private equity funds also have their own specific types of criteria and investment horizons, because they have to return the capital back to their investors.

When you take on private equity capital, you know that there will be an eventual exit. While the preferred holding period is three to five years, the life of the fund is generally no longer than ten years, from the time the raise is closed until the time it exits its last company and winds the fund down. As a business owner taking on VC or private equity capital, you must be comfortable with the fact that you will have an exit strategy. Whether it's an outright sale of your business, a sale to a strategic investor or an IPO, there will be an exit because the VC or the PEG has to return money to its investors.

Is there any kind of financing between debt and a sale of your company in less than ten years? Yes! That's where the mezzanine lenders come into play.

Mezzanine Lenders

Mezzanine capital became the "hot" funding vehicle as banks and other lending institutions tightened their criteria after the bubble burst in 2000. Mezzanine capital occupies the place between equity and debt. I call mezzanine capital "patient" capital, because even though, like bank debt, you will be paying interest on the money you borrow, mezzanine lenders really want to see their investment grow and will take warrants as part of their deal so that they participate in your company's growth.

Mezzanine investors typically are very risk tolerant. They will closely examine a company's current and historical financial results with a particular eye to cash flow in order to determine if the company can afford to pay off the unsecured debt they are offering. A typical mezzanine position in a company's capital structure will be junior (subordinated) to all senior and any collateralized debt positions.

Mezzanine lenders charge a fixed interest rate on their money, usually between 12 percent and 15 percent, and expect to be paid quarterly interest. Sometimes the interest will be paid in kind (PIK) and sometimes it will accrue, but in any event, be prepared to pay a much higher rate than you would at the bank for the "bet" the mezzanine lender is willing to make on you, your management team, and your growth strategy.

By maintaining a flexible structure and augmenting the debt terms with warrants or some other equity feature, businesses find a lot of flexibility in attracting this type of capital.

Mezzanine funding may be used for buyouts, recapitalizations, acquisitions, and fueling growth past a point at which a senior lender would feel comfortable but below the level an equity investor would be willing to provide.

■ REMEMBER

Mezzanine funds are going to charge you a much higher interest rate than a bank, but unlike a private equity investor or VC that takes a percentage of the business up front, mezzanine investors use their warrant coverage on the back end to make up for the risk they took on the deal, meaning that they will have the reserved right at their discretion to purchase your company's stock at a certain time, at a certain price.

While the VCs typically want a 35 percent annual internal rate of return (IRR) and private equity looks for IRR of 25 percent to 35 percent, mezzanine players are satisfied with a return someplace between 18 percent and 25 percent, because they will be earning interest on their capital along the way, thereby mitigating their long-term risk. So, mezzanine lenders can be viewed either as cheap equity or expensive debt.

You can see that all these players are interested in aggressively growing your company. Why would you, as the owner of a closely held business, want to take on this kind of investment? If you are an empire builder, you cannot grow your company aggressively without additional infusions of capital. This kind of growth cannot happen organically.

An entire book could be written about all the hybrid deals that combine debt with equity lending. It's very complicated. I don't want to make this chapter so complicated that your eyes glaze over and you fail to follow its advice. While I understand the many layers of this complicated financing— I've been doing deals like this for 20 years—that's not what this book is about. If you understand debt options the way I've explained them and you understand the information in this chapter, as you go through the process of recapitalizing your business, you will learn. And, hopefully, you'll be smart enough to go ahead. Chapter 8 outlines all the advisors you need to grow your business. Don't think you can do it alone. This book gives you a nice road map, but this is a very complicated and sophisticated subject and you need to employ the best people to help get your business where you want it to go.

WHEN YOU VENTURE AMONG THE CAPITALISTS: WHAT IT TAKES TO CONVINCE AN INVESTOR OF YOUR HIGH-GROWTH PLANS

Venture capital funds typically are run by investment professionals who have a fiduciary responsibility to their investors and thus pay strict attention to the companies in which they invest with regard to corporate housekeeping, business planning, management team-building, internal projections, document preparation, and due diligence. How this information is presented in the proposal can be critical to a successful capital raise.

Your Written Business Plan

When you approach any potential equity investor in your business, you need to present a written business plan that has the following components:

- *A brief executive summary.* This is an overview of your business, no more than one or two pages in length. This summary's purpose is so that the potential investor can read it quickly and get a very good idea of where you are going with the money you seek. If you can't describe your business and its objectives in two pages or less, you don't have a clear vision of your venture and you might as well go back to the drawing board
- *Opportunity overview.* This is your assessment of where your business or service will be positioned in the marketplace
- *Financial component.* This section should detail how much money you need and where you'll spend it
- Detailed biographies of your key management team
- A clear path to how you'll make money
- Potential exit strategy

Business plans are very difficult to write. The financial piece alone—all the projections and analyses—takes thought and possibly a lot of input from professional financial analysts.

As an owner of a closely held business, you might also turn to a lawyer and friends to help you with this process. For one thing, it's very difficult to be objective about something you are passionate about, and if you are starting a business or raising money to expand your current business, what seems crystal clear and important to you may not make sense to someone on the outside. You may not realize that your explanations don't make sense or don't play to the needs of the investor or the marketplace. You need outside readers to give you feedback about what works with your plan and what isn't working at all, so that you don't run into the same bump when your potential investors are reading your plan.

Nine times out of ten, you are introduced to investor groups as a "favor" to a friend of the owner, CEO, CFO, etc. This a highly *ineffective* way to raise funds; moreover, after several months of talking with investor groups and getting nowhere, your business might appear tired and shopworn—as much as one tries to be discreet, eventually Wall Street has a way of knowing who's out there knocking on doors.

Finding the Right Fit

Raising capital is an extremely time-consuming and labor-intensive process. Selecting, engaging, and working with well-respected and experienced outside advisors, other counsel, bankers, and auditors early in the process can be crucial to a successful raise. Remember, an investor group of venture capitalists probably looks at 100 or more companies a year, so your request for funds and your company must stand out.

Do as much research as necessary to ensure that you understand the VCs' focus and their investment objectives. VC funds produce exceptional internal rates of return for their investors; this is how they stay in business and raise capital for future funds. A successful venture must be able to meet or exceed the group's internal objectives—as a guideline, typically a 30 percent or higher annual return.

The next most important point is to know what your business is worth. As mentioned in Chapter 2, many business owners who create their own companies just don't believe they have an ugly baby! But, as we discussed in Chapter 4, not understanding how your company is valued by potential investors is probably the single biggest deal killer. The value of your company must be based on solid financial information. You must know how comparable publicly traded companies are valued, what mergers and acquisitions have been going on in your industry, how to value your future cash flows through discount cash flow (DCF) analysis, and the historical growth rate of your industry as well as the projected rate. In each of these areas, the most compelling details will be those that make investing in your company too good to pass up.

Industry focus is another important investment criterion. Funds often are focused on a certain market sector, such as consumer products, technology, biotechnology, and media. Your investment opportunity must fit within your investor's industry focus. It also is essential to know in advance how much money your investor actually has to invest. An investor or investment fund with $250 million to invest will have a hard time justifying a $5 million venture, because doing the due diligence and working with that company takes the same amount of time and effort as a $20 million investment. It's simply not prudent for that lender to work with $5 million at a time and then stay on top of the activities of 50 different companies in which it has invested.

Additional factors that should be investigated before presenting to an investor group are:

- *The stage of development of your company.* Are you looking for seed capital or are you in a later stage of development?
- *Funding round.* Is this your first round or a later round of capital?
- *Geographic location.* Many investors have criteria around specific areas of the country in which they are able to invest.

Nuts and Bolts

In my experience, business owners often forget that wealth creation is best achieved by focusing on executing the plan to build a successful company rather than by puffing up your ego while nitpicking valuation issues and ownership interests. From the VC or lender's perspective, nothing is higher on the priority list than management, management, and management. Management with a strong, proven track record and relevant skill set is the most important factor in evaluating an investment. How your management views the business and their own contribution, experience, industriousness, and commitment and willingness to work with new partners are all factors that can further a positive result.

In preparing for the meeting, always keep in mind that the business plan or confidential information memorandum you create, as with all forms of communication to potential investors, must present the company in the best light. Be sure all documents are credible and accurate and that they cover every aspect of the company the potential investors may query: the opportunity and market size and segments; all variables including customers, technology, distribution, and competition; management skills and experience; marketing strategy and sales plans; strategic relationships; and current and projected financials. This information must be clear and able to stand up to the strictest due diligence examination—and help you present the business opportunity in an enticing and compelling manner.

Navigating the Process

Many companies seeking funding never obtain it. One of the reasons for this is what I call the "entrepreneur's curse": they like to do it themselves, their way! But seeking outside advice is nowhere more critical than when bringing outside investors into your company.

The multitude of corporate governance issues that need to be addressed in any financial venture fairly demand the assistance of a skilled attorney, and the same principle may be true in terms of a lawyer's knowledge of business capitalization. Don't be hesitant to secure outside guidance that might benefit you. Engage an experienced and objective investment banker to help determine valuation and structure and to review—or even present—the company financials if this will help. Raising capital signals an exciting time in a company's development; the trick is in increasing the odds of obtaining it.

HOW A RECAPITALIZATION WORKS ($ IN MILLIONS)

- In a recapitalization, the owner sells a portion of his or her entire ownership to a financial sponsor. This enables the owner to diversify personal net worth by taking most of the "chips off the table," while also maintaining partial ownership in the business going forward, achieving "the second bite of the apple."
- The entity is recapitalized with (1) new bank debt and (2) equity capital from a financial sponsor.
- In our illustrative scenario (below), the owner sells 90 percent of her ownership to a financial sponsor (who puts up $18 million) for 25 percent in the newly recapitalized entity ($2 million).

Total Enterprise Value:

Net Debt to Be Retired	$ 0
Equity Dollars Contributed by Financial Sponsor	$18.0
Equity Dollars Contributed by Owner	$ 2.0
	$20.0

Recapitalized New Company (NEWCO)

Equity Dollars Contributed by Owner	$ 2.0
New Bank Debt (assumes NEWCO has $4 million in EBITDA and received debt funding at 3.0 EBIDTA)	12.0
New Equity from Financial Sponsor	6.0
	$20.0

So here's what happened: The financial sponsors put up $18 million, but then leveraged the company, which means they've taken their $18 million out and replaced $12 million of it with bank debt. They now have $6 million of cash—their own cash—to use in other transactions and $12 million of bank debt in this transaction, because they know that it's better to put leverage (debt) on this deal. They are confident that the cash flow generated by NEWCO will be able to service the debt and pay the bank back on schedule. How do they know? The company has historically had good, strong EBIDTA; it's never missed its revenue targets. Let's say the business generated $4 million a year cash flow; that would be about a $20 million valuation (the company traded at five times EBIDTA, hence the $20 million) so it would have to have four times EBIDTA. At three times EBIDTA, which is the size of the debt and a figure they *know* the company can achieve, they know that's where they get the ability to take on $12 million in debt.

Leverage recapitalization seems very murky and mysterious and difficult, but it's really very easy if you know that the company has good cash flow and solid prospects for future growth.

So now the financial sponsor has new equity in the deal of $6 million. The business owner has $2 million, and they have to pay the bank back $12 million.

THE SECOND BITE OF THE APPLE ($ in millions)

The owner's equity ownership in NEWCO, or the $2 million initial investment, is positioned for substantial growth as the positive impact of leverage begins to accrue over time. In this scenario, the owner's $2 million investment grows to approximately $6.1 million at exit.

In this scenario, the owner:

- Maintains an interest in a business she knows very well
- Can potentially defer taxes on capital gains and enjoy significant upside potential
- Ends up with a substantial gain, while also taking significant cash off the table from day one

Equity Dollars Contributed by Owner	$2.0
New Equity from Financial Sponsor	6.0
25 percent IRR over 5-Year Hold Period	
Owner's Equity Dollars Become	6.1
Sponsor's Equity Dollars Become	18.3

The 25 percent IRR means that's by how much the company is growing and it has been growing at that rate over a five-year period. That means that the $2 million that the owner has in the business becomes $6.1 million; the $6 million that the private equity investors had in the business becomes $18.3 million; and they've paid off the bank debt. And now you can do it all over again!

Debt is leverage—that's why it's so important to under-stand how to use debt and how to put leverage on a company. That's why it's wrong *not* to leverage at all. You don't want to overleverage, but if you don't leverage at all, you are leaving all of *your own money* on the table. For the business owner, you are leaving all this equity in the business at risk when you could be taking out that money and pocketing it as cash for use in other investments or however you wish.

The catch is that the equity investor and the owner have to be totally sure that the business will generate enough money to pay back the debt. How do they know?

They've researched the company and they know what rev-enues it generates. Nothing has surfaced to spook or scare them. They have done three months of due diligence and nothing has come out of left field that could impact earnings and could make them worried that they might uncover some-thing else bad in the earnings profile. The company has had repeatable, sustainable earnings. That's why the banks are will-ing to lend to the company—its earnings are not just a one-time phenomenon. It has a solid management team that the banks are confident will keep earnings on track. The company has a solid business plan that everyone—the bank, the private equity guys, and the owner—thinks is executable. It has a his-tory, a plan, and solid management—all of these things are credible and all are real.

There may be market forces that they can't predict, but that's the risk in any deal. As an investor, you have to be savvy and careful. That's why market cycles matter. You have to be opportunistic and you have to understand what it takes to get you to the next level. Know when to hold them and when to fold them. When things are going along in a very robust way, if you don't want to take some chips off the table, you need to ask yourself, can you withstand a downturn? Can you withstand a flat market? What is it going to take to get you to the next level?

When you are doing your SWOT analyses, market forces are one of the things you have to look at externally.

CHAPTER SIX

When to Hold Them, When to Fold Them

THE LIFECYCLE OF A BUSINESS

If you've read this far in this book, chances are you are an empire builder, not a lifestyle maker. Perhaps one of the most difficult challenges that empire builders face is understanding that businesses, like people and plants and other growing things, have their own lifecycles to which attention must be paid. Some empire builders have no trouble developing a plan and sticking to it, and that includes the plan's exit strategy. But many owners of closely held businesses find letting go very difficult. Why?

This business is their baby, their vision, and part and parcel of who they are. Not only their capital, but their very identity, is tied up in their business. They may have had huge success, but the question they must always address is, do I have what it takes to grow my business to the next level? This chapter outlines what those levels are and what it takes—financially, logistically, psychologically—to make the leap up.

As I've said repeatedly, if your business isn't growing, it's dying, and you need either to plan for a merger, an acquisition, or IPO; to reinvent the business from the ground up; or to exercise your exit strategy sooner rather than later.

This chapter addresses a very important issue in the lifecycle of any business: the owner's state of mind. For the empire builder who doesn't know what to do next, this chapter offers the tools he or she may need to move the business up to the next level or get out with a sense of purpose and peace, and to appreciate what it takes psychologically to decide between these two options.

LET'S REVIEW: THE STAGES OF A BUSINESS'S LIFECYCLE

All businesses have a lifecycle and there's an optimal time to sell. The optimal time to sell a business is when it's on its way up, not after it has hit its peak and is on the way down, because potential buyers want to buy the dream and the future.

Let's review your business's history.

Start-up. You go from zero to a point where you are cash-flow positive and you can get financing to fuel your growth.

Early-stage growth. Different from starting up, this is where you are taking on some outside capital in order to stabilize your ongoing concern.

Well-capitalized business. At this stage, you may have taken on bank debt, equity, a mezzanine investor, or a few silent partners or angel investors, and you are shooting for the moon. For most empire builders, this is the fun part, where you are working your plan and creating value in your company. You are building out your infrastructure and building up your management team. You understand your markets and actually are executing your business plan. You are not building a business anymore. You are in business. You are in the groove. During this time, you should be figuring out how you are driving the value of your business every single day.

Mature business. You reach a point where you will need to do something very major to get to the next level, because you know if your business doesn't grow, it dies. You must buy a very large company, take on major partners, or exercise your exit strategy because you've done all you can do at the current level.

Exit strategy. You realize you want out, not up. There's nothing wrong with that, as long as you've planned for it.

Leaping the hurdle. If you decide instead of exiting to go for the next level, you essentially go back to the iteration of early stage growth, because you will have to put all your money and resources back into the business. At this point, you won't be generating enough financial growth inexpensively without bringing in outside capital. You will lade the

balance sheet with debt or take in more equity and recapitalize the business for that next leg up. You have to do the equation of time and money. If it took you 20 years to grow from
$0 to $40 million, how long will it take you to reach the next
level and is it worth it? Can you weather another business cycle? Markets are cyclical. You need to be aware of what's going on in the business environment and in your industry.

The homebuilding business is a good example. When the
economy is strong and interest rates are low, people feel
good about taking on larger mortgage payments and second
mortgages. That drives the entire building products industry.
When the market begins to turn, it turns very quickly. If you
haven't sold your building goods business on the way up, you
will have to wait for the next market cycle for another
chance.

Another good example is technology. When the economy is very good and people are willing to invest in their businesses, they are going to invest in technology. A lot of new
equipment can be financed to fit their cash flow. But when
the market starts to turn down, they won't be able to keep investing in the technology in order to leverage their business
to the next level. They have to make sure they put infrastructure in place, so that if their earnings go flat for a while, the
cost of the new technology leveraging isn't going to drain the
business.

We don't know how long market cycles are, so this is
where you also have to factor in the personal side of it. A lot
of things get in the way of continuing:

- Outright fatigue of running the business
- Age of the business owner

- Life and family issues
- External factors such as changes or consolidation in your industry

There are a lot of reasons why you might not be inclined to take a business up to the next level; for example, confluences in the industry, where consolidation could make it very difficult for you to compete. Are you willing to reinvent yourself? If you want to go out and look for the next great product to manufacture, that's one option. A good example can be found in the IT services and staffing industry. When technology came about and people started these companies, the margins were very nice. But there were very low barriers to entry into this field: Anyone who understood the technology and knew how to work on the equipment and solve the problems or resell the equipment could hang a shingle. Then some experts in this field got more sophisticated about running this kind of business, bought up a lot of small companies, and also started to develop bigger, much longer-term, and more complicated and sophisticated problem-solving technologies, which then created bigger margined business that also pushed the little guys out. The little guys who were not willing to be part of the roll-up and who were not willing to sell during that upward trajectory in that market rode past the peak to find the margins eroded out of their businesses. Now, IT services and staffing is a very low-margin business in general.

If you had an IT services and staffing business ten years ago and foresaw the business cycle in this industry and had the foresight to sell out to a competitor, you did well. But if you hung on to your business and did not continue to grow it, you probably only are scraping by now.

I talked to a man recently who is in document imaging, and the same thing is going on there. What's important now is e-documentation, not copying. He runs all these copy centers for law offices nationwide, but it's become a low-margin business. I suggested that he might want to get rid of it, but that's not the kind of entrepreneur he is. Copying is what he built his business on and he is having a hard time transitioning to the bigger-margin e-documentation business. What he's doing is plowing all his profits from this low-margin business that is becoming extinct into funding new technology for this bigger margined business, so his earnings are down. Meanwhile, companies who were smarter about it and got ahead of the curve are being bought up at very big multiples and his business is taking a dive right at the time when he could be reaping big bucks. He's weathering it while he tries to figure out where to take his business next.

Here's a way to visualize the most important factors in a business's lifecycle:

- External: What's happening externally in the industry; external market factors
- Internal: Your business's actual lifecycle itself
- Personal (overriding) issues: What do *you* want to do? Where do you want to take business? The personal factor is what distinguishes closely held private companies and *Fortune* 500 companies that exist in perpetuity.

My document imaging entrepreneur is one kind of entrepreneur: one who wants to dig in and grow to the next level. But there is also another kind of entrepreneur, a very particular breed of entrepreneur—and often a very successful one.

THE SERIAL ENTREPRENEUR

Some entrepreneurs *love* to start things; once they get the business up and going, they are ready to move with their next great idea and start something else. We in the investment world call these people "serial entrepreneurs." Their modus operandi is "start, sell, start, sell" ad infinitum. These are not necessarily your lifestyle makers; they can be very serious businesspeople who form and work their plan and have a clear exit strategy. Serial entrepreneurs know how to start things and know how to get a business up and running, but once their vision is realized, they are ready to move on.

In the lifecycle of a business, it's actually quite rare that the person who starts the business is the one who takes it to its final glory—the IPO or whatever. That's because people who are very good at starting things are not usually great at running mature businesses. There is a very different skill set involved in each process. As the start-up person, you are chief cook and bottle washer and do everything, including the scraping together of resources. When you have a more mature business—one that has resources, people, and capital—you have to manage it all. Serial entrepreneurs have the energy to start up but they don't usually have the patience to manage an ongoing concern. In this mature stage of a business, entrepreneurs must take on a much more strategic role and leverage with people underneath them. Some visionaries like that process, but in my experience, most don't. There are other breeds of entrepreneurs who know how to manage and leverage and love doing just that. They may not be able to come up with a creative business idea, but they have different skill sets and interests and love to roll up their sleeves and solve the problems that take a company from early stage growth to maturity.

This chapter addresses both kinds of entrepreneurs.

At some point, as you reach that mature stage with a seasoned management team and a stable business, how do you get that next leg up? You might be tempted to go to the next level, but think again.

THE QUESTION OF CONTROL

Most people's image of entrepreneurs is that they like to be in control. How do you stay in control of your business?

For some business owners, giving up control is a big problem, because they don't know how to do it. Control and the matter of trust are key issues in knowing when to hold on and when to move on.

Inability to give up control is the main reason why some business owners are serial entrepreneurs. They like to take a business approach to a certain level, perhaps to the point where they have cash flowing in regularly and they've really created some value in the business, but they simply aren't comfortable with someone else running the day-to-day operations.

If this picture describes you, it's time for you to exit from your business and turn it over to someone who is comfortable growing it to that next level. You need to start a new endeavor in which you can once again be in complete control.

There are certain readers of this book who will never be able to grow a business at all. They will start and sell and start and sell, and may never reach the point of being able to bring in partners in an operational capacity. Is that an accurate description of you? If so, you must realize that you'll kill the business if you don't get out of the business's way, because at some point, it will get too big for one person to manage alone and you won't have put in place the team necessary to take over.

Here's a good analogy: If you live in a 600-square-foot apartment, you can be the chief cook and bottle washer, but if you have a 54-room mansion on ten acres, you simply can't do it all yourself. You need staff to help you.

Just because you can start up a business and can run it for a while does *not* mean you are good at managing staff. When you start to scale or leverage a company, when you start to experience—or have the potential to experience—tremendous growth, you are going to have to become a manager and you will not be able to control every aspect of your business. Not everybody can let go.

WHO DO YOU TRUST?

Here's a difficult question: You've started your business and want to grow with it, but how do you make that leap to trust someone else to manage your baby on a day-to-day basis?

A lot of entrepreneurs never make that leap to grow their businesses to maturity and beyond because they can never get to that trust factor. They think they know what they're doing; they make the leap and hire a manager without doing their homework first—in other words, they are not clear about what skill sets they need at any one stage of growth. Many of them bring in someone *just like them,* for instance, and become embroiled in clashes and fireworks over—you guessed it!—issues of control that interfere with getting any work done at all, never mind the real work that must be done to grow a business. Or they might bring in someone at the opposite end of the spectrum, a person who is not like them— someone too rigid, who doesn't fit into the company culture, perhaps a person who needs to be somewhere with tremendous infrastructure, which is not where your business is at this point. If it's growing and changing too fast, that person will get lost and not be able to function.

When you are in this in-between period—high growth but still early stage (not mature)—you need to have someone in operations that has had previous experience in running companies, but who also understands the entrepreneurial nature of a closely held business. This kind of person is very tough to find. It's a very competitive slot to fill. Where do you turn?

Finding the Right Talent

The types of people you can look to for talent include other entrepreneurs who have exited their businesses and consultants.

People who have exited mature businesses.

These people may have cashed out and are looking to come back in and bring another business up to that next level.

Consultants. People who have come from the consulting world are a good source of talent. Often they've seen, analyzed, and worked in lots of different types of businesses. They can be very good in positions like this, or they can lead you to exactly the right person you need.

At every stage of your business, get in the habit of using outside consultants. At start-up when you can't really afford a professional board, create your own board of advisors, people who are rooting for you, know something about business, and want to help. You're not going to have the money to pay them, so you need a group of people who want to help you and with whom you can share and shape ideas.

As the business matures, you might want to create other stakeholder positions in the form of a board of directors, for instance, to help you govern and make the right kinds of hiring decisions. In fact, if you take on outside capital, you will get a board of directors, because the people who invest in your company—private equity investors, VCs, or mezzanine lenders involved in your business—will want you to form a board and give them one or two seats on it.

You are going to have to be accountable to these investors, because no one will want to put their time, energy, and resources into helping you grow your business if they don't have input about how to do it.

This comes back to control: If you want to be in total control and you want to be the one running the whole show, you might not ever take on a board, but then you'll have a lifestyle business and you'll stunt your company's growth.

FREE TO BE *ME!*

At some point, you have to separate yourself from your business. We talked about this in earlier chapters. The business can't always be you and all about you. At some point, it has to be its own entity, its own persona. It's a significant step in the lifecycle of a company when the owner, creator, visionary realizes that his or her talents may not be adaptable to the business's changing needs. Some parents homeschool their kids, but the majority leave that piece of their kids' maturity cycle to someone else—education professionals who specialize in teaching kids at all stages of physical and intellectual growth. It's no different in business: different talent is needed in all stages to help the business mature. That's why at some point you, the owner, must remove yourself from personal loans to the business, take capital out of the business, and secure a nest egg for yourself. Why is financial security important? Because you are financially secure, you make different spending decisions than when you are not—in life and in business. When you are secure, you are willing to get rid of some of your low-margin customers and focus on the higher-margin business, even though it might be hard to land or might be on a longer business cycle, because you know that you have the staying power.

It takes a very objective, self-aware, mature, sophisticated thinker to be able to separate himself or herself from an on-going concern and let other people do the things that he or she is not capable of doing or cannot do well. Often a recapitalization is the way business owners begin to extract themselves both financially and emotionally from the business. With some chips off the table and your financial future secured, you can begin to take a much more critical view of your company. You will also have a board of directors to help guide you as well.

TRUST FROM A DIFFERENT PERSPECTIVE

The point of having money and a well-capitalized business is so that you understand where you are from your constant SWOT analyses, and you are using that capital to bring in resources. When you do, you are releasing yourself to function at the highest potential possible. That means if you are the company's visionary, you can continue to do what you love knowing that someone else is worrying about the financials.

Take, for example, my friend, shoe designer Taryn Rose. She has a background in podiatry and orthopedic surgery and also an interest in and flair for fashion. Her vision was to invent attractive, high fashion shoes that are also comfortable. And she's the person to do it: she has the technical background that she marries with her passion for flair. However, she doesn't necessarily have the skills or the interest to run a $50 to $100 million company to make this vision happen. While she may be the best visionary for her company, that doesn't mean she is the best person to manage all the support she needs to keep the business going.

Another example is Michael Dell. He is famous for his just-in-time manufacturing, meaning his company builds computers as you order them so it doesn't have to keep tons of inventory on hand. As a result, its overhead was less than, say, that of IBM, which built computers and then offered you what it had available. If IBM didn't have exactly what you needed, you went elsewhere and the computer you didn't buy stayed in IBM's inventory. But soon everyone started following this just-in-time model, and Dell's market advantage disappeared.

Sometimes business owners don't realize that their big market advantage has become commoditized. When that happens, you face a problem. That is why you constantly need to be looking around at the competition and learning what's going on in your industry. If you are not analyzing where to grow your business, then, as previously stated, your business is dying.

If you are just treading water, something is going to come out of left field and you will have a very unpleasant surprise. In business, you can never rest on your laurels. You need to know what unpleasant event is happening in your industry and plan for it, around it, and out of it with a good exit strategy.

THE ENTREPRENEURIAL SPLIT

The entrepreneurial split comes down to, are you a visionary or are you a manager? Usually, the owner of a closely held business isn't both—it is *very rare* to find that combination in one person.

Have you ever spent any time with successful business owners who didn't tell you about their right-hand person—the person in their shop who keeps the trains running for them? They are speaking about their operations person.

People who think out of the box—those who have that gene that allows them to see the future and go for it no-holds-barred—have a different thought process and way of functioning than the person who can dot the I's and cross the T's, manage the cash flow, analyze the working capital needs, and those sorts of things. That's a full-time job for an operations CFO. Both kinds of thinkers and doers are necessary for an ongoing business concern. One is not more or less valuable to the company than the other.

To refine the matter further: as the business grows, that operations CFO probably isn't the salesperson your company needs. Nor is that person the marketing person. You need someone out there who understands sales and can close the deal and bring in business. The person who has the vision might not be a "closer."

You need to have these different layers of people in a business that's growing toward a goal. At some point, you have to realize where your passion lies and be realistic about your shortcomings and find talent that complements your vision.

HOW DO COMPANIES TEND TO GROW?

The first real hurdle is from start-up to $1 million in sales. The next big jump is to $5 million in sales—and that's a big jump.

Beyond that, to get from $5 million to $10 million is going to be very difficult unless you understand your balance sheet, how to get money from the bank, how to finance your working capital, and so on. To get from $5 million to $10 million profitably, with good earnings margins, you have to get rid of the low-hanging fruit in your orchard in order to finance this kind of growth. That means that the low-margin business that got you started when you needed customers to make your vision real is now weighing down your business. Even if that customer has been with you since day one, you need to cut the tie and focus on higher-margins areas.

As your business grows and moves up, your profit margins matter a whole lot more. Your profit margins always matter, but in the beginning you need critical mass to establish your identity and credibility as a business. You need to know in the beginning that people want to buy your products or services; you need their feedback about what you're doing right and doing wrong. As you mature, you want to have a base of better, wider, smarter-margined business and you must be willing to let go of the low-hanging fruit.

When you reach $10 million in sales, the rubber meets the road. Now you really have to analyze where your business is going, and how you're going to get it over the next hurdle to the $20 to $25 million range. It will be virtually impossible to leap to this level without bringing on key management members. At this stage, you must decide:

- Do I want to continue to be in this business?
- Am I really prepared to grow this company further?
- Is this what I really want to do or am I just accustomed to this lifestyle?

On the Road to $25 Million: Get Out of Your Own Way!

If you have decided to continue to grow the business, you need to consider:

- Who really should be on the team?
- What will their jobs be?
- Who's my best and highest potential talent?
- How do I get out of my own way and bring in the right person or persons to get the company moving?
- Where is this exponential growth going to come from?
    - Expanding geographically?
    - Adding a new product line?
    - Finding a new distribution channel?

This is where you have to do some very key SWOT analysis, because you can't go in 14 different directions; you have to analyze whether the person who started you down one path is the person to take you to the next level. Suppose you have a company with a fantastic brick-and-mortar retail business but no Internet presence. You don't know anything about selling on the Internet, you have no direct marketing experience, and you've never ventured into outlets such as QVC, so you might have to hire someone with this set of skills. If you decide that you need to expand your product line, you're going to have to figure out what products to add and find someone who can accomplish this for you. In other words, you have to figure out what is needed for your business to grow and then hire the right people who will bring you to the next stage of growth.

Entrepreneurs make a big mistake trying to boil the ocean, meaning they try to expand on all fronts at once. They think the way to grow exponentially is to increase their product offering and also expand geographically, so in the same month they will add two new products and three new distribution channels. No single business owner can possibly execute all these initiatives at once, or execute them well.

With smart SWOT analyses and smart hires, you reach $25 million in sales. Then what?

The $50 Million Level

Your next hurdle is that you want to get to $50 million in sales. This is exponential growth we're talking about. A lot of people don't like to be in business at this level, because at this point you are spending a lot of time analyzing and researching, and your mistakes become more crucial when you are working with bigger numbers.

Look at it this way: If you are jumping over a one-foot-tall hurdle, it's no big deal if you trip. You may stumble, but chances are you won't be hurt much if you fall. However, if you trip over a four-foot-tall hurdle, the chance of injury is much greater.

If you stumble at $1 million in revenues falling to $900,000, that 10 percent drop is going to hurt, but not as much as a 10 percent drop when you're at $50 million—that's a loss of $5 million. Your problem becomes exponentially bigger than it was at the lower level. So you've got to be *more* analytical and *more* critical; you've got to use more intellectual capital. More brains than brawn are now driving your business, and more business acumen and less entrepreneurial spirit. For certain business owners, the demands of this stage of growth can be a drag. If they're not willing to turn over this day-to-day control to the people who absolutely love this aspect of growing a business—and believe it or not, there are people who absolutely love this stage!—the business will founder right then and there.

$100 Million—and Beyond

As you grow from $50 million to $100 million in revenues, your next big leaps are going to be to $200 million, $250 million, $500 million, and $1 billion. And the elements that correspond with those leaps include:

- The level of talent you have in place
- The different types of capital needs that are available to you
- Opening up of markets geographically
- The ability to grow through M&A, as well as organically

It all begins to tie in: You don't see $500 million companies, no matter how entrepreneurial, without a seasoned management *team* and geographical growth. They've probably done some M&A along the way and they've taken on outside capital in one form or another, either through IPO or private equity—you don't reach this level organically.

When growing plants, in addition to regular watering and pruning, you need to know when they need a boost of fertilizer, and you have to use the right fertilizer for each type of plant. You don't want to feed your rose bushes houseplant food because it may not properly nourish the rose bushes and promote their growth. On a more complex level, the same is true when growing your business. You need to add the right elements at the right time to grow your business.

How do you choose the correct "fertilizer" to grow your business? By *always* doing your SWOT analysis. Smart companies are always analyzing where they are and where they need to go, because they understand they can't control the pace of their opportunities. You don't want to wait to look for organizational consensus at the moment an opportunity appears because while you're trying to figure out what to do, the opportunity will disappear. Smart companies surround themselves with information and are working as a team, and the management is constantly talking about what the company needs to do next. When an opportunity appears, these companies are ready to move and already have their goal in sight.

They've already thought through possible scenarios and determined:

- In the case of an acquisition, here's how we would find the capital for it.
- If we decide to expand geographically, we think it's easier to do so by acquiring a company already in that location rather than to try to build out in another territory.
- If a top sales manager becomes available, here's what we will offer to get him or her to join our operation.

A smart company's management team has these conversations *all the time,* not just once a year at the company getaway picnic. They discuss opportunities every day.

What happens in stagnant companies—those that are not growing and will eventually die—is very different from that of growing companies. Growing companies don't believe in magic or luck. Company A grew to $500 million while Company B got stuck at $10 million before the owner eventually sold to Company A. Both entities started out as the same kind of company. But Company A's CEO wasn't just lucky, she worked smart. She or someone she hired knew what to do and when to do it. She hired the talent she needed. When Company A got stuck, it hired good consultants or sought out the right advisors. It wasn't averse to investing in more human capital, which is a key issue.

Smart companies always know where their weaknesses are—and are able to correct these weaknesses with just the right mix of talent and resources. How do they know? Because they complete SWOT analyses regularly—daily if their industry is growing rapidly.

ONGOING CONCERN, ONGOING OWNER: PLAN YOUR EXIT

Right now we live in a very interesting time. As I write this, Bill Gates has just announced he's stepping down from running the technology company he built, having just missed opportunities to be an innovator on the Internet and having to play catch-up, rather than leading in that area. It's time for a new visionary to take over Microsoft and lead it to its future. Bill Gates just turned 50; he's beginning a new and very exciting and important chapter of his life, but running a multi-billion-dollar company is not part of it. I'm sure part of his thinking was: I've been there and done that. What's next?

Long ago, he realized his vision: A personal computer on everyone's desk and in everyone's home. Now he has a different vision and the means to pursue it: eliminating disease among the world's children. Will he accomplish this? If anyone can, he will.

The point is: He built a highly successful company and he's stepping down so the company can grow to the next level. Gates understands he's not the guy to do it; Steve Ballmer and Ray Ozzie are the ones who will carry on. Could Gates do it if he wanted to? Probably, but not necessarily, and the question is no longer relevant. He's on a different path now.

If you trickle that impulse back down, you've got to know when to hold them and when to fold them. Your good instincts drove you to start up your business. Your good instincts plus your great management team plus your SWOT analyses will guide you into the next stage—up or out. Chapter 7 explains those processes.

TOP TEN EXIT PLANNING MISTAKES

1. *Timing.* Waiting until you must sell.
2. *Being reactive instead of proactive.* Waiting for buyers to come to you.
3. *Having a narrow focus.* Not considering all liquidity options (i.e., MBO, IPO, sale to a financial buyer, recapitalization, outright sale).
4. *Distraction.* Taking your eye off the ball. (Exit planning is a full-time job.)
5. *Valuation.* Not knowing what your company is worth.
6. *Lack of vision.* Not thinking ahead to what life will be like post-exit.
7. *Taxation.* Not thoroughly planning for the impact of taxes.
8. *Improper use of resources.* Not using advisors to your advantage.

(continued)

TOP TEN EXIT PLANNING MISTAKES

9. *Lack of deal experience.* Not understanding what happens or needs to happen to complete the transaction.
10. *Deal drag.* Taking too long to complete a transaction and causing the buyer to lose interest.

CHAPTER SEVEN

Doing the Deal

So you are seriously thinking about going into "fold them" mode; that is, you are ready to exit your business. You still run an ongoing concern and, as a matter of fact, the business is going quite well right now. But you've done your SWOT analyses and studied the business climate, and internal and external indicators tell you the company is at a point in its lifecycle where cashing out, or at least taking some chips off the table, is the smart thing for you to do. Your thinking about what brought you to this point might include the following:

- You are feeling the toll of running a cash-constrained business. Selling to a large, well-capitalized entity that can unleash your company's untapped potential may be very appealing. You'll gain access to ready capital and a strong industry network with the right buyer. You may lose control over the day-to-day operations but by relinquishing some operational control your company is getting the resources it needs to move to the next level. If you stay involved, you'll probably find yourself spending more time on the aspects you enjoy most and less time "in the weeds."

- Your executive team has done a fantastic job but the company is stretched in terms of how it can reward its key employees. Selling to the large well-capitalized entity offers your employees better job security and a brighter financial future. Losing key talent at this stage is a real risk if you can't provide compensation and benefits in line with industry standards.

- Industry trends are starting to look hazy over the long term. Smart sellers know that the time to sell a business is when the company is on an upward trajectory, not when it's turned a corner and is on its way down and perhaps missed something.

- Your major product or patent risks becoming obsolete. Having flown under the radar screen of the top guns while you were small, you've managed to grow to the point that you are perceived as a threat or worse—a company they could seriously challenge or even bury by throwing money at your company's product or service and doing it themselves.

- You don't want to be naive by not seriously considering the degree of real and potential competition in your evaluation of the timing of the sale or recapitalization of the company. That's what buyers and investors do all the time when they evaluate building, buying, or investing.

- You can't forget the simple timing of market forces. One of the interesting things that's happening as I write this chapter in mid-2006 is that so many closely held businesses got through 2000 and 2001—a very difficult time for such entities—but for the last several years, the economy has been healthy and there's ready capital to fuel business growth. With business booming once again, many business owners may think, "Hey, business is going really well. Maybe I shouldn't sell now." But think again. If it took you 10, 15, or 20 years to grow your business and the market timing is right for *now,* consider how much more you'll have to grow to make it worth the wait. At least consider taking some chips off the table through a recapitalization when market conditions favor sellers.

When in doubt, go back to your SWOT analysis and closely examine, unemotionally, if the now is the right time to exit your business. If an exit is your next step, do you know who would buy your company and why?

This chapter examines the steps you should take to prepare for your exit and what you can expect from the deal process that leads you to your exit.

POTENTIAL BUYERS

First, let's take a look at who the potential acquirers may be. Generally, they fall into three categories:

1. *Strategic buyers.* These can be your competitors or larger corporations both public and private that understand that growth through acquisition is a viable strategy. We also see suppliers, vendors, and customers buying companies to enhance their growth or eliminate the middleman.

2. *Financial buyers.* These can be private equity funds, merchant banks, or venture capital groups who are looking to purchase a company and then grow it in a meaningful way so they can cash out and realize a return on their investment.

3. *Individual buyers.* These may either be wealthy entrepreneurs who are looking for their next opportunity, employees through vehicles known as ESOPs (employee stock option plans), or management buyouts.

Each of these buyers will be looking at much of the same critical information in order to determine if the acquisition is a smart one, but each will have different objectives and criteria for deciding to bring the deal to fruition.

Strategic Buyers

Strategic buyers tend to take the long view of business life. Many times these are companies that have been around for 30, 40, 50, or more years in one form or another and so they look to find companies that can help them benefit in the long haul. The most common reasons a company makes a strategic acquisition is to enter a new market—either geographically, or by adding new products and services to their mix or gaining access to new distribution channels.

Often we see companies on the acquisition trail simply gobbling up market share—somewhat akin to a land grab—as another driver for a strategic buyer to pursue an acquisition.

Acquiring a new technology or system will make the deal happen, especially if the company has determined that the technology could become a barrier to entry if it doesn't have it. Sometimes a large corporation will buy out its smaller competitor just to eliminate some of the competition.

■ REMEMBER

Smart companies are always evaluating their options. Larger entities that have growth through acquisition as a major initiative will often employ their own corporate development people whose job it is to strategize and go after certain companies in certain target markets. Also remember that companies that are serious about growth through acquisition are talking about it. It is a part of their business strategy and they are ready to act when the right opportunity comes down the path.

It goes without saying that a strategic buyer will be looking for synergies and if the company doing the acquisition is public, it will be virtually impossible for it to get board approval unless a strong business case can be made for the additive nature of the deal.

Financial Buyers

Financial buyers view an acquisition a bit differently. They are looking to make an investment and expect to get a return on their investment (25 percent or higher annual IRR) over a very specific time horizon, usually three to five years. Financial buyers look for opportunities to use their capital and resources—whether those resources are other portfolio companies, executives in residence, or experienced management teams—to create profitable exit strategies.

■ REMEMBER

A private equity fund is made up of investors who are looking for real cash returns on the money they have put up to portfolio managers (general partners) to invest in private companies.

Individual Buyers

Your own employees, through an employee stock option program (ESOP), or your senior management team, through a management buyout (MBO), financed by a private equity firm who "sponsors" the team (hence the term "financial sponsor") can be a good alternative to running a formal sales process.

TO HIRE OR NOT TO HIRE: THAT'S THE QUESTION

Selling your company takes the kind of thought, selection, and commitment that you would make when you decide to get married. Without the desire and a commitment, you'll never get to the altar. If either the bride or groom fails to show up on the wedding day, months, maybe years, of preparation have been wasted and there's bitterness on both sides. Running a sales process is long, arduous, disruptive, and can be highly emotional; it is best left to professional advisors.

What do we mean when we say "running a sales process"? You need to understand this process because you can't get the best outcome—sale, recapitalization, or financing—unless you have the right information prepared and you approach the transaction in a professional way. While you don't want to run the deal process yourself, the more prepared you are about what's expected of you and what will happen as you move forward, the better informed your decisions will be.

Once a company becomes serious about putting itself in the market, the owners and any key senior management (or any "over-the-fence" people) should begin the interview process for a qualified investment banker. Spend some time interviewing different firms. Talk to small boutiques and larger companies. You will want to find out what experience the bankers have in working with companies of your size, in your industry, and at your stage of development. And don't be afraid to ask for references.

Investment bankers can be a critical factor in determining whether or not a transaction actually makes it to the finish line. If you are even exploring the possibility of a sale of your company, it is a good idea to have some introductory conversations with bankers to get an outside perspective into what's happening in the current M&A market. You need to talk with bankers who do deals every day to determine if your expectations are in line with current market trends and to determine their interest in taking on your assignment. Because the majority of their fee is based on closing the deal—their share at closing is often called the success fee—good investment bankers will not want to become engaged in a transaction they do not believe they can effectively close, and usually you can gauge their interest in the enthusiasm of their "pitch" for your business. If you don't feel they are doing an A+ job of selling you to hire them during their pitch, ask yourself if you think they can really get behind you and your company and convince others to give you the best price and terms.

When you hire a banker to run your deal, you send a message to the prospective buyers that you are serious about selling. Running a strong process, which is what the bankers do for you, requires a disinterested third-party advisor who can unemotionally sort through the various issues at hand.

Here are some other points to consider in deciding whether or not to hire an investment banker:

- You, the business owner, already have a full-time job running your company and that should continue to be your number one priority. The worst thing that can happen during a sale process is to have something go wrong with the business. Selling a business is also a full-time job that takes a team to run a sell-side process smoothly.

- Investment bankers understand business valuation and how to present both the high points and potential issues in the most flattering light. Remember, these are people who have lots of knowledge about various valuation methodologies and pitfalls, and can perform analyses quickly and accurately while keeping the process on track.

- Most likely the potential transaction is something you will want to keep hidden so that you don't have unnecessary disruption of your business or word leaking out to customers and competitors. Investment bankers can act in your interests without having to name your company until they determine whether a potential buyer is serious. Remember: that potential buyer could be your biggest competitor and it's in your company's interest to control the release of information.

THE DEAL PROCESS

Once you have engaged a banker, you both will sit down and agree on the actual process that will be used to sell your company. Generally, the process follows one of three methods:

1. Negotiated sale
2. Broad auction process
3. Modified auction

A *negotiated sale* is what happens when you have a very small universe of buyers, usually fewer than five. A lot of times there are only one or two buyers who actually come to the table. It is not unusual for a company to call and tell me that they have been approached and are seriously considering an offer. In that case, we have to determine if the company wants to explore other potential suitors or simply proceed with the suitor at hand. If you choose to go down the path with only one or perhaps two or three prospective purchasers, then you would be entering into a negotiated sale.

There are many benefits to dealing with only a handful of the most logical buyers:

- It is easier to keep the transaction highly confidential.
- You can remain very flexible in your negotiations, timing, and dissemination of information.
- Business interruption should be minimal.

But on the downside:

- It's hard to create a real horse race—a competitive situation—so you risk leaving value on the table.
- It's tough to create a sense of urgency, so the deal can drag or die a slow death.
- If you don't end up closing the transaction, you have invested time and money with no return.
- If for any reason news of the failed deal leaks out, then you risk your company appearing "shopworn" to new suitors.

A *broad auction* is exactly the opposite. This deal process is evident when you pick up the *Wall Street Journal* and see that a company is for sale and everybody knows about it. Anyone who has the financial wherewithal to pay for the company can offer to buy it. This is the best way to drive to the very highest price on a deal. However, it's also the best way to let all your competitors, customers, and employees know that the company is in transition. If you contemplate a broad auction sale, you need to get an investment banking firm involved, because you've got to ensure that this transaction comes to a conclusion. Why? Because if you should not close the sale, every headhunter is going to be out there talking to your employees and all your competitors are going to be wining and dining your customers, and your company could lose its valuation very quickly.

In a broad auction, your object is to create an extremely competitive environment where anyone with the financial wherewithal to buy the company can come to the party. In this instance, it is widely known that your company is on the market.

The advantages of a broad auction include:

- You can create tremendous price competition in this scenario.
- Often, a buyer who you hadn't even considered may throw its hat in the ring.

The disadvantages, however, are formidable:

- Every employee, customer, and competitor knows that your company is up for sale, which means that your employees are entertaining thoughts of what might happen post-deal and offers of employment elsewhere, your competitors are selling against you by preying on the easily perceived uncertainty of your future, and your customers are wondering who will be taking care of them in the long haul.
- When you run a broad auction process, you lose a lot of the flexibility that was open to you in a highly negotiated transaction because you need to maintain as much of a level playing field as possible. You must disseminate the same information to all parties, receive offers in a timely fashion, and conduct the due diligence process in a professional and highly structured way.
- You need a financial professional to run a broad auction, because this type of process draws the truly serious deal-doers out of the woodwork. They are low on patience and won't commit resources (time, people, and money) to proper due diligence if they don't believe you are running a serious deal process. For this reason, this is a process generally for larger deals handled by an investment banker.
- Should you, the seller, fail in this process, you have a very serious problem on your hands: the company is now viewed as "tainted goods" by the business community at large and, closer to home, by every employee, customer, and competitor. They all now know the story.

A *modified auction* is the deal I like best for closely held businesses, because you have the best of both worlds. In this deal process, you are marrying the best qualities of a negotiated sale and a broad auction.

The advantages to a modified auction include:

- A limited number of participants (usually no more that 20 to 30) who are prequalified by your investment banker for appetite (desire to do a deal) and the financial wherewithal to get the transaction closed
- The ability to carefully control the dissemination of confidential information
- A high degree of flexibility—you can start with a small number of participants (around ten or so) and expand the process as you and your bankers see fit
- Minimal business disruption—only the owner and the "over-the-fence" members of management will know what's happening
- Potential to receive maximum value—with 10 to 20 players, you can create a horse race and can drive the sales price up. Even if one or two potential buyers drop out, you still have others at the table to keep the process moving.

As in the other two scenarios, the disadvantages of this process include:

- It takes time to complete.
- It puts the company under the microscope of potential competitors.

- If for some reason the transaction is not completed, it can damage the reputation of the company.

■ REMEMBER

No matter how hard a company tries to keep things quiet, any time management exhibits odd behavior, employees are going to wonder what's up.

Once you've decided what kind of process you'll run, review the steps you need to take to make sure you'll get your desired outcome: a successful sale or recapitalization.

PREPARING FOR THE SALE

The three most important things to remember when you decide to make the leap and expose your company to potential buyers or investors are *preparation, preparation,* and *preparation.*

Even before engaging an investment banker and going to market, it is important to prepare. In most cases, you need to go over your financials, which hopefully have been audited carefully by a reputable accounting firm. Shore up any gaps in business planning, and make sure that as you move through a deal process, which may take up to a year, your company isn't going to have any issues that will rear their ugly little heads at the wrong time and delay or derail the process.

If you own the business outright, through a trust, or with investors or other family members, now would be the time to evaluate the tax implications of various types of sales—for example, an asset versus stock purchase. Seeking the advice of the right accountant and tax and estate planning professionals is critical to you, the business owner, in achieving your expected outcome. It will be virtually impossible to sort thorough personal details or restructure assets at the same time the deal is trying to close, so get that planning out of the way first and know what your goals are for the sale.

Due diligence. After you hire an investment bank, there will be a preparation period in which the professionals who will be marketing your company to prospective buyers will need to understand every aspect of the business. Their inquiry will not be limited to financial data. Your banking team will want to know all there is to know about your sales and marketing, who your top customers are, how long you've had them, and why they buy from you. They'll want to dig down into your day-to-day operations and understand what happens on a micro level and how it affects the big picture for the company. Interviews with key management will also be part of the preliminary due diligence process as information is gathered that will be used in writing the confidential information memorandum.

See the sample due diligence checklist at end of this chapter, and note how extensive the bankers' inquiries are.

List of potential buyers. While due diligence information is being compiled, a list of potential buyers will also be developed. It is wise to ask to have input on this list, because you may know of some ready buyers, including competitors, who have previously approached you. The bankers may also list companies that you would never sell to if your life depended on it. It is better to refine the list up front, so you and the bankers are on the same page.

Confidential information memorandum (CIM).

The primary method for disseminating information to prospective purchasers is through the CIM, but there are a few steps that are taken before much confidential information is handed over. Typically, a teaser and an executive summary are developed in tandem and used to gauge a buyer's level of interest in your company. The teaser will give enough information about the company for a buyer to decide that the profile sounds like something it could be interested in. If indeed that is the case, the buyer will then be asked to sign a nondisclosure agreement (NDA) or confidentiality agreement (CA). These are legal documents that are enforced to help ensure the trustworthiness of the company that will be viewing your sensitive and confidential information.

It is worth mentioning that companies who are in acquisition mode have pretty tight parameters on what they will and won't sign off on. For instance, if you ask for the confidentiality agreement to be upheld in perpetuity or over a ten-year period, it will probably be returned unsigned. (Can you remember what you talked about ten years ago?) So it's in your best interest to create a strong but reasonable document ready to go so the process isn't unnecessarily held up in a negotiation to get information!

Executive summary. Once your bankers have signed NDAs in hand, they will send out the executive summary. At this point, the company name is revealed, as well as its background, business description, and high-level financial information.

If the buyer still remains interested, then the company will ask for the CIM (commonly referred to as "the book"). As noted above, this document delineates all aspects of the company's business. Major sections include a company history, industry overview, historical and current financials, business plans and strategy, details of real estate and facilities, customer relationships, and management bios.

Gauging interest. As the process moves on, the bankers will begin to gauge interest from the questions that the prospective buyers are asking. In response, you can expect your investment bankers to work with you to put together a presentation that you will give to the interested parties. While the bankers set up the meeting and stimulate the buyers' enthusiasm about the opportunity, ultimately the time spent with you and your team will create the excitement and sizzle.

You will find too that at this point interested parties may want to come out to the company and kick the tires for themselves. They're looking for those "intangible extras," the plusses or minuses that make or break a deal. It's easy to hide worn machinery or poor facility management in a document, but one walk-through will tell an experienced buyer if something is not quite up to snuff. Likewise, it's not hard to get a sense, especially through body language, about how an employee or key executive is feeling.

The data room. While all of this is going on between bankers, buyers, and management, a data room is being built. This is where your prospective purchasers will go to see for themselves what your financials, employment agreements, customer contracts, leases, and other written commitments look like. After this review, they will come back with their questions and concerns and may want to meet with management.

Indications of interest and the meltdown. At some point, usually after there are enough parties at the table so that one buyer walking out doesn't tank the deal, the bankers will set a deadline for indication of interest. These will be formal letters with nonbinding indications of price and terms. This is what my friend and colleague, Debi Larrison, fondly calls the "tension convention," and it's a good description of this moment when the business owner's years of blood, sweat, and tears are boiled down into one concise statement of price and terms. It can be a very emotional time for the owner. Try to remember two key things here:

1. There's a price and then there are terms. Try to stay flexible so you can achieve your personal financial goals.
2. It's not what you get but what you keep that matters, so don't hesitate to have your tax advisors help you navigate terms at this stage.

The negotiation. At this point, the negotiation begins and you will really appreciate the importance of having an experienced investment banker at your side. Eventually, the offers will be boiled down and one will be accepted. When that happens, there will be a stated deadline for the close and whatever further information the buyer will want to receive.

Papering the deal. Now is the time that your seasoned M&A legal counsel comes into play. A definitive purchase agreement will be drafted and negotiated and you, the business owner, will also be required to make representations and warrants about certain aspects of the business. If not papered properly, terms in this document could come back to haunt you.

OBSTACLES TO THE CLOSING

Most of the time, if you get to this stage you can advance the deal over the finish line. There are, however, certain factors that can get in the way. These can include:

- *Employee retention issues.* Who will be staying or leaving post-closing? Are there any stock options or other compensation that kicks in if the deal closes?
- *Key customer contracts.* At this point, you will probably need to let your customers know what's happening. To whom do these relationships really belong—the company and your brand or the salesperson who deals with

the buyers on a day-to-day basis? Will these relationships remain even if the sales contact is replaced?

- *Financial reporting issues.* Are there any issues that the
  auditors have raised? Is the deal's back end in place?
  Have you or your CFO used any accounting "tricks"
  that the buyer may not consider in a favorable light to
  make the numbers look better? Are you hitting your
  plan? Now is the worst time imaginable to miss your
  numbers.

- *Incompatible cultures.* Of all the things (price and terms
  aside) that kill a deal or create a post-deal integration
  disaster scenario, this is the biggest. Companies that
  run like a top—employees report in at 8 AM and out at
  5 PM and take two weeks of vacation; hold regularly
  scheduled meetings; and have written policies, procedures, and plans to follow—will find themselves in a
  very unhappy marriage if they try to merge with a truly
  entrepreneurial culture that runs on flex time, closes
  for two weeks at Christmas, and conducts meetings
  over the ping-pong table in the break room.

- *Potential liabilities.* It is important to come clean about
  any potentially negative situations—legal, environmental, or otherwise—that could cause undue future harm
  to a buyer. Putting these issues on the table up front so
  that everyone is clear about the risks associated with the
  transaction can save you a lot of time and money in the
  long haul. Many issues can be worked around and
  taken into consideration in the final deal. For instance,
  if you have a legal problem and may face settlement
  costs, funds may be escrowed. Remember too that you
  will be making representations and warranties about

the company. You don't want to face a lawsuit because you incorrectly represented a situation.

- *Inability to agree on valuation or the deal structure.* There's your price and then there are terms. Make sure you understand before you go to market what your valuation range will be and how the terms most likely will lay out.

CLOSING THE DEAL: SAYING "I DO"

If you make it through the sales process, obtain the purchase agreement that the lawyers have tinkered with and approved, and everyone has signed on the dotted lines, *the deal closes.* There's a big party, like a wedding reception, you drink great wine, everyone's very happy, and that's that. You sold to or married players who have hearty appetites and the resolve to say, at long last, "I do.

Those two words complete the lifecycle of your business. What's next for you in the process of capitalizing on your success?

THINGS TO REMEMBER WHEN YOU DECIDE TO SELL:

- Timing is everything.
- Determine the company's worth.
- Hold the "tax people" at bay.

(continued)

THINGS TO REMEMBER WHEN YOU DECIDE TO SELL:

- Engage the necessary advisors to help with the transaction.
- Know how to prepare the company for sale.
- Acknowledge that the buyer is the biggest, most important customer.
- Show your company's true, maximized earnings.
- Know where to find the best buyers.
- Outsmart the sharks by negotiating price and terms the *right* way.
- Know surefire deal structuring methods.
- Avoid the inevitable legal traps.
- Anticipate the buyer's due diligence investigation.

PRELIMINARY DUE DILIGENCE CHECKLIST

Financial Statements

- ❐ Past three years audited projections
- ❐ Copy of any current business plans or multiyear projections
- ❐ All operating plans, statement of capitalization, and budgets and projections, including capital addition plans

Other Financial Documents

☐ Current offering document(s), if any

☐ Detailed schedule of operating expenses for past year and for first six months

☐ Detailed schedule of other income (or other income/expense) for past year and for first nine months

☐ List of loans to and from officers, shareholders, directors, and employees with interest rate(s) and repayment terms

☐ Schedule of dividends paid over last three years

☐ Loans and lines of credit agreement

☐ Summary of off-balance-sheet assets and liabilities (e.g., nonoperating assets, pension plans, warranties, pending litigation, and other contingent liabilities)

☐ Synopsis of leases for facilities and equipment

Corporate Documents

☐ Copies of articles of incorporation (received), bylaws, and any amendments to either

☐ Stockholder list with shares held and a brief description of the stock if more than one class of stock exists (voting/nonvoting, preferred, etc.)

☐ All long-range, strategic, and marketing plans

☐ Summary description of employee benefit plans

- ☐ Copies of shareholder agreements, buy-sell agreements, employment contracts, noncompete agreements, and any other contracts

Operating Facilities and Other Assets

- ☐ List of all significant operating facilities, including sales breakout by location
- ☐ Schedule and description of nonoperating investments, including appraised values
- ☐ List of any additional assets that may be considered temporary or not directly related to the company's normal operations (nonoperating assets), with an estimate of value

Products/Markets/History

- ☐ Brief history of the company
- ☐ Copies of recent marketing materials, sales brochures, catalogs, or other descriptive sales materials, including articles on the company
- ☐ Unit volume and/or revenue analysis for existing products, product lines, services, or service lines for the past three years
- ☐ Top ten (or more, if appropriate) summary customer analysis, including sales and/or unit volume for at least the last three years
- ☐ Major accounts gained/lost during the past two years with actual and expected future sales
- ☐ List of major competitors

❐ Summary listing of the company's major competitive strengths and weaknesses, by major area/product/location or other categorizations, if applicable

Operations and Production

❐ Any company patents, trademarks, or licenses that facilitate its business, with a description and indication of their "value" from a marketing or competitive viewpoint

❐ Copies of any available industry or trade association studies or surveys showing comparative financial and/or operating performance

❐ Details of contracts relative to leases, suppliers, customers, and franchise or distributor agreements

Management/Personnel/Board of Directors

For key personnel, provide:

❐ Annual compensation, including bonuses for three years and expected total compensation for current year

❐ Name, title, age, and years of service with the company

❐ Current operating responsibilities and a brief description of past operating responsibilities, if different

❏ Brief description of any relevant industry experience outside your company

For all employees, provide:

❏ Total number of full-time and part-time at year-end for the last two years
❏ Names, start dates, summary of education and experience, classifications, skill sets, and general wage scales

Marketing

❏ Customer base and demographics
❏ Number of clients
❏ Repeat customers
❏ How product moved through the sales channel (e.g., distribution methods, such as direct sales, inside sales, mail order, online, distributors, trade shows, seminars, conferences)
❏ Number of sales personnel (inside/outside) and their compensation
❏ Corporate advantage with marketing

Operations

☐ Facilities: location (e.g., business park, stand alone, downtown, etc.), leasing terms (e.g., expirations, rent, assignable, if applicable), real estate

☐ Competitive advantages

☐ Vendors and subcontractors of parts/services, including contractual relationships and agreements

☐ Efficiencies/economies of scale

☐ Cost competitiveness

☐ Additional capital requirements

Industry Trends and Forecasts

☐ Market size

☐ Growth rate of industry and maturity of industry (evolving/stagnant)

☐ Attractiveness of the industry (e.g., growth, service lines, sex appeal)

☐ Chief characteristics of industry and impact on business

☐ Drivers of change in the industry and the impact on business (e.g., new companies, technologies, products, innovations, changes), pricing

Competitive Analysis

- ❐ Key competitors
- ❐ Factors on which the competition is based
- ❐ Impact of competitors (negative or positive) on the market
- ❐ Key factors to competitive success
- ❐ Whether competitors' services are similar or highly differentiated

It Takes a Village

I love to buy fine things for my home, but every once in a while I hire an interior decorator to give me some advice. She comes over and whizzes around my house and makes comments like, "You need a little height over here, some additional spot lighting over there, something chunkier in that corner . . ." and she transforms my space into something more functional and inviting. When I hire her, I'm not admitting that I don't have a good eye or good taste. I don't lack a sense of style; that's not the issue. I recognize she has a talent I don't have to bring my vision to another level and I'm happy to pay her for her services and advice.

In our personal lives, we have no problem bringing in outside experts to help us manage day-to-day chores. Those who don't have a sense of taste or proportion will call in an interior decorator or designer without a moment's hesitation to help them with the function and appearance of their living space. People who like fashion but don't have a sense of style will hire a personal shopper. Others hire landscapers to make their properties look beautiful. Even people who refuse to read a recipe can still throw wonderful parties by hiring a party planner and caterer—and take all the credit for the fabulous time their guests have. Why? Because they know how to hire professionals to help them manage the areas in their personal lives that they have no time or talent to attend to.

For some reason, though, when we get into business, we resist the concept of using outside talent to make our companies work better. Why? We have lots of excuses:

- It's expensive.
- It takes time to find the right people and establish trust in their capabilities.
- We give up operational control, which feels like we failed.

What we fail to appreciate, though, is that when we hire the right advisors, we have someone with whom to share our vision and are able to execute it within their sphere of expertise. In doing so, they can bring the company to a new level of profitability and growth.

It does take a village to run a company. You do need to go outside for a lot of different reasons: for perspective, to find people who can refine your vision so that it's doable, and to confer with people who can fill in where you have holes or blanks or gaps in your plan.

THE ISSUE OF CONTROL

Why aren't entrepreneurs open to outside expertise? They have a mistaken notion that by doing so, they are giving up some control in the running of their companies—and they are not wrong in that notion. What they fail to see, however, is that by giving up some control, they actually wind up with *more* control, because the reality of running a company in today's complex business environment is that it's a complex process. It's impossible for one person to keep all the plates spinning, and to attempt to do so could cause everything to spin *out* of control. When you try to manage too many things and you are not the best person at executing everything, you actually *lose* control over important aspects of your company. If you bring in the right people at the right time to help you, and you align yourself with their advice, you maintain control over your organization, your products and services, and the outcome.

Every entrepreneur needs people in whom they can place their trust and who can execute for them. And that's why it takes a village to run a company properly.

This chapter focuses on external professional service providers who can make an extraordinary impact on your time, management, growth strategy, and outcomes.

INTERNAL/EXTERNAL

So far, much of our focus has been on work that happens inside an organization as it grows and how to make sure you have the right resources (people and money) to ensure your success, but it takes more than good internal talent, motivation, and vision to move a company forward in a meaningful way. It takes aligning yourself with the right service providers and organizations to which you can outsource critical projects and technical issues.

Again, you must go back to your SWOT analysis: You've got to be able to look at your business world internally and externally. The "village" of external people from which you can get help is going to change at every stage of growth.

WHO TO HIRE AND WHEN

How do you decide who to hire at each stage? The answer is simple: economics. You hire the best people you can afford at every stage of growth. You need to know what kind of capital you have to support your outside people at every level. When you begin, you need an array of informal advisors who are rooting for you and are out there to help. As you grow, you want dedicated people, but the way to get dedicated people is by paying them for their services. Serial entrepreneurs—who start businesses, run with them, and then cash out—have a lot of capital to put back into their next new venture and have their outside people completely teed up. These entrepreneurs have an advantage over a business owner who is starting from scratch, mortgaging his house to invest in the business, or financing parts of the business with a credit card. It follows that you need capital to get a business where you want it to go. You don't want to be spending money frivolously on outside advisors. For instance, you don't need to pay for audited financials until you are starting the process of getting loans, until you are ready to raise capital, or until you have significant cash flow; however, right from the get-go, you do need the assurance that someone has structured your business in the right way. Therefore, you need to invest in superb legal advice from the beginning.

Suppose your company should have been set up as a C corporation but you structured yourself as an S corporation or an LLC. That mistake could come back to haunt you later if you ever decide to tackle a recapitalization or growth through acquisition. Likewise, if you've added real estate into the business instead of keeping it separate, that could be something that interferes with a transaction down the road. Investment bankers frequently see a business's early-stage planning mistakes at the worst time—when they're trying to close the deal! When that happens, we have to stop the current process or transaction and fix the problem (which is expensive and time-consuming to do) before the process can move forward.

This problem can be avoided if you keep focused on these questions: What's your vision for the business? What's your plan? Having papered your business with the correct legal documents, you can be confident that your vision is intact as the business grows.

Let's look at the outside people you should look to for help as you grow your business.

Advice Early On

It is beneficial to find someone who can help you develop your business plan and a financial business model when you are creating your business. *Who* can do that?

- Professional business plan writers
- Experienced business people in your community
- Business accountants or other financial professionals who can make sure you are setting up your books and records properly

Help as You Start Up

It might be good enough to have a bookkeeper and use software packages such as QuickBooks or Peachtree to manage your accounting. That way you can turn over the files to your CPA at tax time and he or she doesn't have to spend hours trying to reconcile a year's worth of work. You are not making a lot of money in the start-up phase, so it is a good idea to outsource these functions because you don't have to issue complicated tax forms and you don't have a big payroll to meet.

Legal documents need to be in good shape from the beginning, although at this point you don't have a lot of partners or investors, so you don't have to worry about having very technical documents that have a lot of moving parts to them and include a lot of "what-ifs" and "but-fors" and other legalese that only competent lawyers can translate. But, as mentioned earlier, you do need to have the proper legal framework for your particular business in place so that down the road you do not have to hold up growth opportunities to fix any problems or loopholes in your original plans.

Assistance as Your Business Matures

As you grow, perhaps by taking on a bank loan (there will be a legal document involved), you need to begin to add layers of review. Documents, especially those involving other people's money, must be looked over. You should understand clearly all of your terms and covenants—your promises—to pay back the money (how much and when). What assets are you pledging to secure the loan? Which one of your children have you just pledged to the bank? You are also going to have interest issues, so you need an accountant that understands the different business deductions for your type of business.

Growing to the Next Level with Advisors

If you contemplate any kind of leap in growth, you need to upgrade the quality and quantity of the advisors you seek out for information and services. I divide this village into the following sectors:

- *Financial*—accountants, commercial lenders, angel investors, VCs, and other private investor groups
- *Legal*—attorneys and contract experts

- *Consultants*—executive coaches and interim CFOs and COOs
- *Community resources*—nonprofit business "help" organizations, college and university business courses, and entrepreneurial societies

Let's look at each of these sectors in more detail.

Financial. The level of advisors with which you surround yourself sends a powerful message to commercial bankers, financing partners, attorneys, and consultants—to the entire business community—about your own professionalism and seriousness in their world. I'm not saying there aren't very bright one- and two-man shops that can help, because there are. But if you are presenting audited financials from a known audit firm, the information will be taken more seriously than if your CPA prepares and reviews them. If you are an empire builder in the early stages, you do not necessarily need the services of one of the Big Three accounting firms (Ernst & Young, Deloitte & Touche, or PricewaterhouseCoopers) but you might want to investigate the ones that work with smaller, closely held businesses (there's a whole tier below the Big Three that work with smaller companies, including Grant Thornton, Pannell Kerr Forrester, and BDO Se) because they understand your issues and you send a powerful message to the business community about who is representing you and how serious you are about your business.

View it this way: If your suppliers or vendors are asking you for financials so they can extend you credit, and your financials are prepared by a professional accounting firm they recognize, it shows that you observe industry best practices and they know they can trust the information they see. This is even more important when a bank, mezzanine lender, or private equity investor asks you for this information.

Legal. The same concept applies to the legal help you need. As you get more sophisticated in your contracts, hires, distribution and compensation plans, you need attorneys who are more sophisticated at papering those kinds of deals. If the lawyer who drafted your initial business plan doesn't take into account new business issues that may arise—or, worse, isn't even aware of them—then that one tiny mistake in the contract that you don't catch, or a failure to update a document during a rush of new business, could be very costly for you down the pike.

Particularly if you are considering acquisition as part of your growth strategy, it is crucial that you receive guidance and legal advice from attorneys who are familiar with the mechanics and ramifications of deal making. Very often you face antitrust, intellectual property, or employment issues that you never faced before. A good team of lawyers is essential during a capital raise or IPO to warn you of such threats and show you how to avoid them.

Many people object to paying premium prices for premium services, but the price you pay if you don't use the proper advisors can be far costlier, not only in terms of money but in terms of time and lost opportunity

Let's say you are a business owner generating revenues of $5 million and someone comes along and wants to buy you out. You are probably not going to hire an investment banker at that level; instead, you'll need a good M&A attorney. The reason is economics. Smaller businesses tend to be much better off being brokered, and often the owners find their own buyers or sell to their employees through ESOP plans. They don't need to pay an investment banker hundreds of thousands of dollars to find buyers for them and run the deal process because at that level the process will not pay for itself. What the business does need is a good attorney to paper the deal. You'll have to pay legal fees, and taxes on the transaction regardless of who else is involved, but if the owner hires an investment banker, the owner probably won't net enough to make the sale worthwhile.

Is there a percentage of gross revenues that you should be spending on outside advisors? No, there's no formula. The amount depends much more on the kind of deal you are going to do. But be mindful that as the business grows, it gets more sophisticated and complicated, as in life. When you start out, you get married and you make a will. You are 26 years old and you have some savings and an apartment and that's it. And then children come along and you need a more complicated will to include guardianship issues should anything happen to you and your spouse. As you begin to acquire wealth, you need to have a much more complicated will. The more issues that come along with this wealth, the more sophisticated your will and estate planning need to be. If you get to the big leagues and acquire several hundred million dollars, then you have all kinds of issues—trust, estate, tax planning—that have to be addressed. It's an evolutionary thing. Each new stage requires additional planning.

In your business, do a cost-benefit analysis: If you have $100,000 in revenues, you are not going to spend $25,000 in legal fees per year, because that would not be a wise way to spend the company's money.

Consultants. It's important to understand where and when to go for help. You must avoid letting a business problem spiral out of control *before* you attempt to bring in someone to fix it. You never want to let any aspect of your business get to the point where it needs to be fixed, because it can be very expensive to get you on track again. It's much smarter to be proactive—seek advice on the front end—and hire the right people to help before you get into those kinds of problems.

What kind of help might you need? Consultants can advise you in lots of ways. Management consultants can serve as team coaches who come in and observe you, your executive team, and your operations with an eye to helping you build bench strength internally. Consultants also offer suggestions about staying on track with your business plan and vision for growth, so you don't derail.

Interim CFOs or COOs often fill the critical gap between a bookkeeper or accountant handling the financial picture and someone who eventually becomes a part of the senior management team and understands how to integrate operational issues properly into the financial working of a company.

Outside professionals are much more objective when it comes to helping you analyze change. When you go through your SWOT analysis, it is a smart idea to bring in an outside consultant to participate in those off-site meetings; these meetings are so important and they need good facilitators to keep the discussions on track. Just as it's difficult be objective when you coach your own child in sports, when you ask your executive team to analyze their own organizations, the issues can get very cloudy and you can end up with everyone patting themselves on the back and congratulating themselves for being part of a great company. You don't get a realistic picture of where you are and where your company needs to go. The outcomes of these off-site meetings need to be productive, and a facilitator can help accomplish that.

Outside resources. There are great organizations in every business community where you can learn exactly the kinds of things you need to know, meet other entrepreneurs and business owners, and begin to develop a professional advisory network that can help you grow to the next level. These people would be external to your company and might be connected with such organizations as:

- The Young Presidents Organization
- Women Presidents Organization
- Small Business Association
- Inc. Eagles
- SCORE
- Family Firm Institute
- Industry and trade associations

All of these—plus many not listed—are excellent resources. The Internet is also full of valuable information.

Many colleges and universities have resources available to business owners and entrepreneurs. They may have executives-in-residence who advise community business leaders for a fee or through programs and courses for business executives and entrepreneurs.

A word of caution: don't let yourself get overwhelmed with too much information. You need to learn how to use all the resources available in a way that doesn't waste your time. You lose time gathering information and processing it. If you get to a point where you are wasting time, you lose the focus you need for your business.

Used judiciously, outside resources can be extremely valuable, but you need to target exactly what kind of information you need before you go out and look for it.

ON TO THE NEXT LEVEL

The advisors in your "village" will change as your business grows. Each time you get to the point where you are considering growing your business to the next level, you have to ask yourself, is my entire team—internally and externally—the team that will take me where I want to go?

If you ask that question and realize that your current team is not the right team, you need to look for replacements. For example, suppose you have a bookkeeper or CPA that you've used for years, a very loyal person who knows your business inside out. The business has grown and you are at the point of taking on business partners. You now need a much more sophisticated accounting package, because taxes and distribution of moneys are going to be more complex in a business partnership than in a sole proprietorship. You may need to find an interim CFO and adjust the bookkeeper's role in your organization.

Let's say you want to bring capital or loans into your business, and now you need your financials to be audited. This new business direction will require a level of accounting that a CPA might not be able to provide. You may need to hire an accounting firm that services closely held businesses.

Likewise, when people look at your client contracts or your employment agreements, they get a very good idea about the level of sophistication with which you operate your business—and they will treat you accordingly. So it's very important, particularly as you grow, to consider whether your support people are still serving your business's needs. You may have needed one kind of attorney to get from point A to point D, but at point D, you may need someone else. As you get even larger, you may use one law firm for your employment issues and a different one for your M&A issues. That would not be uncommon.

You may want to hire headhunters to find talent in the beginning, but you may need an executive search firm down the road.

As you grow, who you seek out comes down to this question: What is the best and most efficient use of my time, energy, and resources (money)? It's very expensive in business to make mistakes and, as you grow, exponentially expensive. Having a document prepared incorrectly is costly, and could be disastrous. If you had documents drawn up on the cheap on the front end, it might become an issue later when you get into trouble, when you have a problem, or when something unforeseen arises. When you started out, you might have saved money by hiring legal interns to draft certain documents, but as you grow and the business becomes more complex, you'll pay for any mistakes your attorneys made. And you will be very sorry if you haven't invested properly in protecting yourself and your business.

As your business goes up a level, your level of advisors also has to go up. Yes, better help is more expensive. Many business owners don't want to spend that money, but when they are willing to invest internally *and* externally to put together a top-notch team, the payoff can be enormous. These owners will be more competitive out there in the real world of the big players.

HOW DO YOU KNOW AN ADVISOR IS REPUTABLE?

The answer is simple: network. Ask around. Listen to your fellow entrepreneurs who boast about their right-hand people, the key people they rely on every day, or legal or financial professionals they've consulted with whose advice saved them time and money. Ask what qualities these advisors have that are important to you. Ask how they found these advisors, and then contact the advisors and mine them for information.

RAISING THE BAR

As your business grows, you are constantly raising the bar.

Having a business plan, knowing where you are in your plan, being able to measure it, and constantly talking to people and interviewing them to see where you are and what you could be doing next is the way to run a village—and an empire. This brings us full circle to what was mentioned in

Chapter 1: If you have the right plan, the best people, the top advisors, and the passion, running an empire is far easier than running a village, because you can leave all the difficult day-to-day decisions to your trusted team and have the freedom to think strategically and *Capitalize on Your Success!*

GLOSSARY

asset financing Assuming a lien on equipment, inventory, and accounts receivable in exchange for an infusion of cash to grow a business.

barriers to (market) entry Regulations or lack thereof that affect how easily a new product or service can be offered to the general public or consumer.

bond financing A way to finance certain projects that will benefit not only the company but also the surrounding community by producing jobs and increased tax revenues.

C corporation A business which is a completely separate entity than its owners. Corporation is taxed on earning, shareholders are taxed on dividends. The structure also allows for different levels of shareholders (i.e., common and preferred) and capital is raised through stock.

capital improvements Upgrades to fixed assets (equipment, warehouses, tech systems) needed to stay competitive.

cash flow Repeatable, sustainable revenues. Good cash flow adds to a company's valuation.

Comps (also known as comparable company analysis and competitive pricing analysis) Spreadsheet models that compare and contrast the vital financial statistics of companies in the same industry, such as Nike, Reebok, and Converse. Comps help bankers value a company's financial position relative to others in the same industry by comparing data such as current stock prices, earnings, and financial ratios.

deal The process and completion of a security issuance or acquisition or merger of a company.

debt Money borrowed that will be paid back with interest.

discounted cash flow (DCF) An analysis of future cash flow that discounts it, often using the weighted average cost of capital, to arrive at a company's present value.

due diligence A process that determines the security risk to the lender of a company that is up for sale. The process involves the bankers and their lawyers asking the company's management and their accountants questions that could uncover possible risks, because if the bank issues a security for a company with undisclosed risks and then the business falters, investors could lose a lot of money and the bank could be sued.

EBIT (also known as operating profit or cash flow) GAAP term indicating a company's earnings before interest and taxes. In the case of a company with minimal depreciation and amortization activities, creditors closely watch EBIT, because it represents the amount of cash that such a company will be able to use to pay off creditors.

EBITDA Non-GAAP term indicting a company's earnings before interest, taxes, depreciation, and amortization. This earnings measure is of particular interest when companies have large amounts of fixed assets that are subject to heavy depreciation charges (such as manufacturing companies) or when a company has a large amount of acquired intangible assets on its books and is thus subject to large amortization charges (such as a company that has purchased a brand or a company that has recently made a large acquisition).

EBIDTA margin   (EBIDTA ÷ total sales) Measures the extent to which cash operating expenses deplete dollars gained from total sales.

economic value The price at which a business will exchange hands between a willing buyer and a willing seller, neither of which is under duress to act. (See *synergistic value.*)

enterprise value (EV) A measure of what the market believes a company's ongoing operations are worth, usually the company's market cap plus debt plus minority interest plus preferred stock. This number is important both to individual investors and potential acquirers considering a takeover attempt.

equity market value A company's common stock equity as it appears on a balance sheet; how much a company would have left in assets if it went out of business immediately.

equity repurchase A buy-back of share in a company in order to regain control of the business.

factoring A loan almost impossible to pay off in which large infusions of cash that carry high interest rates are needed before certain selling seasons to produce or purchase inventory; common in the fashion industry.

financial sponsor An equity partner who invests capital to back (sponsor) a management team.

first-stage expansion The first phase of growth of a business after start-up.

GAAP Acronym for generally accepted accounting principles.

gross margin An indicator of how much profit is earned on products without consideration of selling and administration costs. It is calculated off of the income statement as gross profit divided by total sales.

growth capital Money that is invested in a company in exchange for part ownership (equity in) the company.

illiquidity discount The difference between what a company would be worth if it were publicly traded and when it is privately held. Publicly traded companies vital statistics are known; those of closely held companies are not, so a buyer or investor can only estimate their value.

junior debt See *subordinated debt.*

layered financing Different kinds of debt and equity used to grow a business.

lease financing Leasing equipment to run a business instead of buying it outright; analogous to leasing a car rather than buying it.

leverage Another term for debt.

leveraged recapitalization A strategy by which a company takes on additional debt to pay a large dividend or repurchase shares of its stock.

LLC Similar to a limited partnership with some of the benefits of incorporating. LLCs may have an unlimited number of members and are not normally taxed (unless chosen). Profit and losses are passed through to the members, and the members, in return, contribute money or services to gain interest in the LLC, which is how capital is raised. An operating agreement with a designated manager determines management.

LP A business organization with one or more general partners, who manage the business and assume legal debts and obligations, and one or more limited partners, who are liable only to the extent of their investments. Limited partners also enjoy rights to the partnership's cash flow, but are not liable for company obligations.

LTM Acronym for last twelve months.

M&A Acronym for mergers and acquisitions.

mature business The stage in a business's lifecycle where it must either grow to the next level, be sold, or die.

mezzanine financing A hybrid form of OPM that mixes debt and equity, carries a high annual rate of return, and falls between high-risk venture capital and security-oriented commercial lenders. It is used by business owners who expect enormous growth in revenues. Mezzanine lenders offer owners of privately held businesses a bridge between taking on debt and doing an IPO.

other people's money (OPM) Investment banker's term for equity investment in a company.

PE multiple Acronym for price-to-earnings multiple, a ratio that indicates if a stock is overvalued or undervalued relative to its historical performance and relative to other firms. To get the PE ratio, divide the market price of a share of common stock by the earnings per share of common stock for the last 12 months.

private equity investors Lenders who look for companies with good growth history, strong management, sustainable revenues, and a rate of return higher than they can get in the public equity markets.

revenue stream Another term for cash flow.

S corporation Corporation with a limited number of shareholders and only one class of stock. The profits and losses of the corporation are passed through to shareholders directly. Capital is added to the company through stock.

senior debt The money borrowed, usually from a bank, that must be paid back before all other debt a company may incur.

serial entrepreneur A business owner who likes to start up and exit companies, but not necessarily manage them through growth and maturity.

small business investment companies (SBICs) Investment organizations, backed by the federal government, that fund funds, so funds can leverage up. If you have a mezzanine fund and you get SBIC financing, you can leverage your fund for up to three times the value of its assets. For example, if you have $100 million you raise yourself, you'll have $300 million to invest.

subordinated debt Debt that is paid off after senior debt and carries a higher rate of interest because it is considered riskier to the lender.

success fee The fee an investment banker receives upon closing a deal.

synergistic value The value of a business determined by the marketplace that takes into account revenue enhancements and cost savings benefits that a particular buyer receives when that buyer acquires or merges with a seller. See *economic value*.

synergy Linking with a well-positioned strategic partner to help both parties reach their full potential. For example, Company A makes $50 million a year; Company B makes $20 million a year. A banker determines that neither company can reach its full potential on its own, but together both parties could make $100 million a year.

SWOT Acronym for strengths, weaknesses, opportunities, and threats. Usually presented in chart form, SWOT analyses are a way to analyze a company's valuation.

TTM Acronym for trailing twelve months.

valuation An assessment of how much a company is worth; what a business owner could hope to realize from the sale of his or her company.

venture capital (VC) An illiquid equity investment in a privately held company. Venture capitalists, the people who make such investments, look for companies that have the potential for extraordinarily high growth.

working capital The cash on hand needed to keep a business running .

INDEX